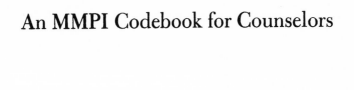

An MMPI Codebook for Counselors

AN MMPI CODEBOOK

FOR COUNSELORS

by

L. E. DRAKE and E. R. OETTING

UNIVERSITY OF MINNESOTA PRESS, Minneapolis

Printed in the United States of America at
North Central Publishing Co., St. Paul

Library of Congress Catalog Card Number: 59-10187

Fourth printing 1972

PUBLISHED IN THE UNITED KINGDOM AND INDIA BY THE OXFORD UNIVERSITY PRESS,
LONDON AND DELHI, AND IN CANADA BY COPP CLARK PUBLISHING CO. LIMITED,
TORONTO

ISBN 0-8166-0187-9

━━━ *PREFACE*

This manual has been designed to assist the trained counselor in deriving, from the MMPI, hypotheses concerning the emotional and attitudinal states of counselees. It may also be of use in the teaching of courses in personality measurement, especially those in which the MMPI is included in the course of study. It is designed, however, for the use of the experienced counselor, and the counselor should be qualified by training and experience before attempting to generalize from the information given.

Although the interpretations are derived from studies of profiles of relatively normal people, they should be useful to clinicians dealing with more deviant persons as well. The constructs accepted by the clinician may be amplified or extended by the constructs based on the codebook materials. It seems reasonable to presume that such extensions will lead to more complete constructs about behavior in general and will provide a rich source for further hypotheses and studies.

We are especially indebted to Dr. Starke R. Hathaway for his encouragement and constructive criticisms. Any weaknesses in design or errors in conclusions are, however, our full responsibility. We are also indebted to Mrs. Agnes G. Young for typing the manuscript, and to Miss Edna M. Hasse for supervising much of the routine clerical work of the original studies.

L. E. D.
E. R. O.

University of Wisconsin
February 1, 1959

───── CONTENTS

The Use of the MMPI in Counseling

THE USE OF PSYCHOMETRIC DATA IN COUNSELING   3

CONSTRUCTION OF HYPOTHESES FOR COUNSELING   10

Scale 0 (SOCIAL INTROVERSION-EXTROVERSION), 15. Scale 1 (HYPO-CHONDRIASIS), 17. Scale 2 (DEPRESSION), 18. Scale 3 (HYSTERIA), 19. Scale 4 (PSYCHOPATHIC DEVIATE), 21. Scale 5 (MASCULINITY-FEMININITY), 22. Scale 6 (PARANOID), 25. Scale 7 (PSYCHASTHENIA), 26. Scale 8 (SCHIZOPHRENIA), 28. Scale 9 (HYPOMANIA), 29. The Validity Scales, 31.

Codebook of MMPI Patterns

INTRODUCTION TO THE CODEBOOK   37

MALE SECTION   40

FEMALE SECTION   73

Appendix Tables

   I. The MMPI Patterns Meeting Statistical Criteria of Significance That Were Shown by Male Students in Each of the Subgroups   127

  II. The MMPI Patterns Meeting Statistical Criteria of Significance That Were Shown by Female Students in Each of the Subgroups   132

References   139

The Use of the MMPI in Counseling

THE USE OF PSYCHO-METRIC DATA IN COUNSELING

Psychometric data may be very useful in counseling. On the other hand, such data at times may lead to more erroneous than correct conclusions. Consequently, before discussing the use of the MMPI, a specific psychometric instrument, we feel it is desirable to set forth a general point of view on the use of psychometric data for counseling purposes.

Practicing counselors vary considerably in their attitudes toward psychometric data and in their use of such data. The Rogerians, for example, believe that testing and the interpretation of test scores interfere with the counseling relationship. At the other extreme are those counselors who apparently identify testing and test interpretation with counseling and place little emphasis upon the counselee's emotional states or his perceptions of his abilities, aptitudes, values, and actions.

The point of view adopted here is somewhere between these two extreme positions. It has been well described by Super in his book *Appraising Vocational Fitness* (19). We do, however, deviate at times from Super's presentation and at other times amplify his position.

We assume that the primary function of counseling is to help the counselee develop a realistic understanding of himself and his relations with the society in which he lives. The counselees dealt with in the educational environment are seldom the extremely disturbed persons found in clinics; for the most part they present the less intense or less crippling problems that are generally characteristic of young people making the transition from late adolescence to adult status. This transition cannot be narrowly defined by age; rather it is that period in the development of the individual when his plans and goals and values are changing from those shaped by transitory interests and fantasies to those determined by more realistic perceptions of himself and his world. At the same time he must develop the social skills and acquire the knowledge necessary for effective living. The young person faced with the necessity of making many decisions even as he is undergoing rapid intellectual, social, and emotional changes often finds himself confused and unhappy. He needs help in developing the realistic self-concepts that underlie maturity.

The achievement of realistic self-concepts is partially dependent upon the young person's having accurate knowledge about his interests, values, and so on, integrating that knowledge into a meaningful picture of himself, and evaluating it in relation to the environment in which he lives or expects to live. Since he is in a state of flux, his perceptions may vary considerably from time to time and may differ from other persons' perceptions of the same factors or events. But in any case it is reasonable to assume that he will perceive more realistically if his observations are based on accurate information.

Some information may be obtained from the person's own statement of feelings and experiences, but other important data cannot be obtained accurately or effectively by this means alone. This is especially true when the data relate to the individual's status within a group. He may feel that he is quite competent in certain respects and make plans for a program of action based on these perceptions. However, unless he has some indication of his *relative* competence, of how he ranks among those with whom he will compete, he will be unable to forecast the outcome of his program with much assurance. If he is a high school graduate and is considering a college program, he may on the basis of his past experiences in schoolwork feel competent to succeed in the college program. These experiences, however, were the result of competing in a population having a wider range of intellectual abilities and with many more persons in the lower ranges than is true of the college population. Consequently he may be in error in his self-assessment. The chances of error are reduced if he knows his relative status in the college group, as indicated, for example, by scores on a college ability test that have been adjusted to college norms. Thus, psychometric data, because of usually higher reliability and validity than other data, and because of the availability of normative tables, can provide useful information for the development of realistic self-concepts that is difficult to obtain in any other way.

The fact that psychometric data are more useful than non-psychometric data in many situations should not lead to undue confidence in such data or in actuarial tables built on them. The actuarial table is based upon groups of individuals, and is supposed to show the relation between some measure of performance and the occurrence of a latter event. Forecasts from actuarial tables may be frequently correct if the validity of the data is high, or only occasionally correct if the validity is low; but there are always misses as well as hits. Whether or not a prediction for a *particular* person will hold up is very uncertain. The counselor must curb the tendency to become overconfident or too certain in forecasting outcomes for individuals — especially when the base rate, or the frequency of occurrence of the event in a population, is very low.

Meehl and Rosen have presented the various aspects of this problem in their article on antecedent probability (18). The problem is particularly pertinent for vocational or educational counseling since the events predicted often occur very infrequently in the population. Suppose, for example, that a test or a battery of tests has been devised to predict which students from an entering college group will become doctors. Suppose, further, that a cut-off score has been established such that 80 per cent of the eventual doctors obtain scores above the cut-off mark while only 5 per cent of those not obtaining M.D. degrees get such scores. This appears to be a very satisfactory set of data for the counselor. However, there is a serious difficulty in the use of this information because the percentage of entering college students that become doctors is so low. Assume that 1 per cent of the entering freshmen group eventually become doctors. Out of 1,000 freshmen, then, the data would successfully predict 8 out of 10 of the future doctors in the class. But the data would also predict, wrongly, that 5 per cent of the remaining 990 students will become doctors. This means that in predicting who will become doctors among these 1,000 students, the counselor would be correct 8 times and incorrect 49 times. In other words he would be wrong about 6 times more often than he would be right.

This problem of predicting relatively rare events is one that must be kept constantly in mind in personality assessment or measurement. A large number of possible interpretations can be made from a profile of the results of a personality inventory. Predictions might be made in regard to criminal tendencies, suicide, psychotic behavior, homosexual behavior, or more common characteristics that can interfere with an effective social or educational adjustment such as sibling conflict and anxieties. Indeed there are so many possibilities that the prediction of any one kind of future behavior on the basis of a personality profile is comparable to the prediction of a rare event. Since such predictions can be more frequently incorrect than correct in any individual case, it might appear that a personality profile should not be used in counseling. However, such an attitude implies that the counselor would not make the prediction at all, or that when he makes the prediction he would do so on a basis that is better than psychometric data. In actual counseling neither of these alternatives is likely to be true. The counselor does occasionally consider rare possibilities. Becoming a doctor or developing criminal tendencies is relatively rare in terms of the frequency of either in the whole population; but since they do occur the counselor from time to time must consider them. Furthermore, comparisons of the accuracy of predictions based on clinical judgments with that of predictions based on psychometric data have found the clinician coming in second best. Meehl in his book *Clinical vs. Statistical Prediction* (16) presents a summary of studies that appear to demonstrate that actuarial tables based upon psychometric data yield better predictions than do clinical observations.

The counselor, then, is faced with the knowledge that a prediction from a test is likely to be better than a random guess but at the same time that he is far more likely to be wrong than correct when making a prediction for an individual case. Since there appears to be no way to improve this situation statistically, the attitude he adopts in the use of prediction data becomes highly important. He cannot assume that he is going to be often correct, because he will often be wrong. Nor can he feel that he is going to be wrong every time, because he then makes no use of the test and hence does not improve on a random guess. His wisest course when making a prediction or diagnosis would seem to lie in regarding the prediction as a hypothesis, a tentative statement that some event *might* take place, or that something *might* be true concerning the individual's adjustments or characteristics. The prediction is a guess, but not a random guess. It has a basis in past experience, frequency tables, and so on. The more valid the observations, psychometric or clinical, the more confidence he may have in the guess. Regardless of how low the degree of validity may be, the method or device should be used until some new method or device or refinement having greater validity is developed. Throwing away instruments or methods because they do not measure up to some arbitrary index of validity when there are no better instruments or methods available means that the counselor is returning to random guessing.

PSYCHOMETRIC DATA IN COUNSELING

However, the limitations of data for counseling, whether the data are objective or subjective, psychometric or clinical, cannot be overemphasized. All the opinions, interpretations, and ideas that the counselor develops about the client, whether as a result of tests or of other observations, should be considered as nothing more than hypotheses that await further confirmation, modification, or rejection as evidence accumulates. The counselor notes a resemblance between the case with which he is dealing and other cases, either in his past experience or in an actuarial table, and then guesses or hypothesizes that the case under consideration will need to be handled in a particular way or will develop in a particular way. Most professionally trained counselors accept the conclusion that construction of hypotheses is the limit of usefulness of data, but in actual practice they may deviate considerably from this position. Regardless of the theory of counseling that the counselor accepts, he should examine carefully the basis of his understanding of the counselee and guard against overconfidence.

The following is a specific example of the construction and modification of hypotheses as a counseling case proceeds. An 18-year-old boy who has just graduated from high school meets with a counselor to determine his chances of success in college. He has been referred by his parents who are especially concerned because the boy graduated in the lower 25 per cent of his high school class. Additional data show that he has a centile rank on a college ability test of 85 (entering freshmen norms), his mother appears to be overly protective, his chief interest has been in building and driving hot-rods, he feels inept with girls, he has a police record for minor delinquencies, and his values are confused and inconsistent.

Actuarial tables based upon rank in high school class and the college ability test show that 70 per cent of the entering students with comparable ratings obtained a C average or better and 30 per cent received an average below C during their first semester in college. The best hypothesis that could be drawn from this table, then, is that the chances are 70 out of 100 that this counselee would obtain a C average or better his first semester and 30 out of 100 that he would obtain less than a C average. If we assume that the college ability test score is an indication of his "academic ability" and relate this score to his rank in his high school class, it appears that he achieved well below capacity in high school. This hypothesis is not based on an actuarial table but depends upon the constructs associated with tests and the integration of the constructs. As such it is useful,

7

although quite removed from simple correlational data, and may lead to the formulation of a new construct that might be labeled "lack of academic motivation." When used to describe the counselee it is an extended hypothesis. Other constructs, based upon the available data, should be examined to determine if they reinforce or modify this hypothesis. The values that may be assumed to be associated with an interest in hot-rods and the acquisition of a police record, the feelings of ineptness with the opposite sex and of rebellion toward an overprotective mother — all may be interpreted to lend support to the hypothesis that the boy lacks academic motivation. We have here a network of hypothetical constructs which go beyond the data but which appear to hold together.

Suppose the counselor now administers the MMPI to the counselee and the resulting profile shows that Scales 9 (Ma) and 8 (Sc) are among the three highest scales, that Scale 0 (Si) is among the lowest scales, and that Scale 5 (Mf) is not high. This particular pattern has been found to differentiate male counselees judged to be lacking in academic motivation. In addition, expectancy tables developed from studies with the MMPI indicate that 67 per cent of male students showing this pattern failed to obtain a C average during their first semester and only 33 per cent obtained a C average or better. This is almost the reverse of the expectancy table based on high school rank and the college ability test score. The counselor may at this point interpret the MMPI data in two ways: they lend support to the hypothesis that this counselee lacks academic motivation, and they also warn that a conclusion derived from the first actuarial table, which points to satisfactory academic achievement, is very uncertain.

Perhaps of more importance is the use of the hypotheses and constructs in the counseling situation itself. For example, the counselee states emphatically that he wants to go to college. Does this statement mean that he has developed a great interest in academic learning, or does it mean that he wants to get away from his home environment or that he sees college as an opportunity for achieving social acceptance? In working out hypotheses and constructs the counselor is made aware of various possible interpretations of a relatively simple statement and can search for information that may help him to decide which interpretation or interpretations are most tenable. Only then can he assist the counselee in the achievement of a realistic understanding of his motivations.

In summary, the counselor constructs and uses hypotheses to the best of his ability in the development of insight and self-realization in the counselee. The hypotheses help the counselor decide on appropriate techniques — nondirective for some counselees, more directive interpretive techniques for others. The counselor must judge not only the benefits to be expected from a particular course of action, but also the problems that might result. The confidence with which he holds a hypothesis will often determine the course that he takes. In working with a college population, test results often allow him to develop the most confident hypotheses and should be an integral part of counseling, although the counselor should not request tests if he feels that such testing might be disturbing or prevent the establishment of good rapport with the counselee.

CONSTRUCTION OF
HYPOTHESES FOR COUNSELING

In the past, the construction of hypotheses from MMPI profiles has been a difficult task for the counseling psychologist. One reason for the difficulty, and also a common criticism of the use of the MMPI with normal persons, is that the original scales were derived from studies of clinical populations and the descriptions of the profiles were couched in terms of deviate behavior, although it was often assumed that the differences between the deviate and the normal person were differences of degree rather than of kind. When a characteristic is so severe as to be disabling, as is often the case in the deviate person, it usually stands out quite clearly. On the other hand, when the characteristic merely modifies a response or action, it may be very difficult to isolate or interpret. Consequently, before the use of the MMPI could be really helpful in counseling, a good deal had to be learned about the implications of the scales for behavior in normal persons.

A second reason for difficulty in interpreting the MMPI lies in the fact that almost all the published work has reported studies of the individual scales. While information about the individual scales may be useful in some instances, the behavior that the counselor is trying to understand or predict is usually too complex to be measured by a single scale. What appears to be a relatively simple characteristic, such as underachieving in academic work, is apparently not related to one scale, or even a combination of scales, but may be related to a number of different patterns of scales (5). Knowledge of these patterns not only is useful in forming hypotheses about individual counselees, but may provide information about the nature of underachievement itself. When such complex patterns are studied, the results are more informative for the counselor than any findings derived from studies of single scales including studies based on routine and unimaginative item analysis, necessary as this kind of analysis is for an understanding of how scales are constructed.

What has been needed, then, is information about the way in which the scales operate in patterns for relatively normal persons. To obtain some such data, studies were carried out at the University of Wisconsin from 1945 to 1957; the codebook section of this volume presents the results in readily usable form. Some of the material on male counselees has been published earlier (3, 4, and 5), but the results of the studies on female counselees appear here for the first time. The procedures and statistics used were identical for both sexes.

We shall summarize only briefly the design of the studies and the weaknesses and strengths of the data; a fuller report may be found in the article "MMPI Profiles and Interview Behavior" (3). Frequency tables and other statistical data on the patterns used in the codebook are given in the appendix to the present volume.

The studies were based on a pool of profiles from 2,634 male students and 1,564 female students. The card form of the MMPI was used. The scales were corrected for K and all profiles judged invalid were discarded. The profiles were coded according to the Hathaway method (7), and frequency tables of the combinations of scale codings were computed for the total groups of men and women. Specifically, the following tabulations were made:

1. The frequency with which each scale was coded among the 3 highest scales.*
2. The frequency with which each scale was coded as one of the 2 lowest scales.†
3. The frequency with which each pair of scales appeared among the 3 highest scales.
4. The frequency with which each pair of scales appeared as the 2 lowest scales.
5. The frequency with which each scale coded high of the 3 highest scales appeared with each scale coded low of the 2 lowest.
6. The frequency with which each pair of scales coded among the 3 highest appeared with each scale coded low of the 2 lowest.

* For a scale to be coded high the T-score had to be 55 or higher.
† For a scale to be coded low the T-score had to be 45 or less.

11

THE USE OF THE MMPI IN COUNSELING

As would be expected from the intercorrelations among the scales on the MMPI, some combinations of scale patterns did not appear, but between 650 and 700 patterns did occur. This seems sufficient for study until a larger pool of profiles is accumulated and more precise methods for observation of behavior are obtained.

Counseling case materials on the students were then read without reference to the profiles; and the problems, descriptive phrases, and other items of information listed by the counselors were compiled. From these, subgroups, or criterion groups, were established — "insomnia," "restless," "home conflict," for example. The profile code for each student was next listed in each subgroup indicated to be appropriate by the case materials on that student. Frequency tables for the combinations of scale codings, like those drawn up for the total groups, were constructed for each subgroup. A comparison of frequencies of occurrence of each pattern could then be made between the subgroup and the total group and the significance of differences tested to determine whether the frequency with which any pattern appeared in a subgroup was greater or less than would be expected from the frequency of occurrence in the total group.

If 20 per cent or more of the total group or the subgroup exhibited a particular pattern and if the difference between the frequencies of the two groups was 2.00 or more times the standard error of the difference, the pattern was accepted as being differential. If less than 20 per cent but more than 10 per cent of the total group or the subgroup exhibited a particular pattern and if the difference between the frequencies of the two groups was 3.00 or more times the standard error of the difference, this pattern was also accepted as being differential.

The number of profiles that could have been assigned to any particular subgroup was probably larger than the number actually so assigned. The reason for this is inherent in the deficiencies of case materials and in the nature of the counseling process itself. Counselors often overlook or omit in their notes behavior manifestations that are important for studies of this sort either because they do not judge the behavior to be important in the particular case or because the behavior may be so apparent that it will be readily noticed in succeeding interviews. Also, the skilled counselor is alert to behavior which might interfere with rapport and uses the techniques at his command to prevent or avoid such behavior. Noticing, for example, a tendency for the counselee to be belligerent, the counselor would be on guard to prevent manifestations of belligerency and, if successful, would not label the counselee as belligerent in his case notes. These factors and others like them would operate to reduce the size of the subgroups but would not increase the validity indices spuriously. The error would more likely be that of reducing the number of subgroups for which differential patterns were found. In the present studies, there were 33 subgroups for which patterns were found that differentiated the male students, 37 for the female students.

A more serious weakness, as far as the validity of the studies is concerned, is the possible "contamination" of some case materials. That is, at times an MMPI profile was in the case folder before the first conference, and the counselor thus may have used the MMPI results in assessing the student's problems and characteristics. This happened because occasionally in busy periods a counselee had to wait for an appointment and in order to use the time advantageously he was tested before the first conference. Even this weakness may not be too serious since the profiles and the case materials were collected before hypotheses had been formulated regarding profiles of normal populations as represented by university students. No counselor presented in case conferences, staff clinics, or seminars interpretations of profiles which could be easily related to the findings of these studies. In fact several of the counselors were opposed to the MMPI and had it administered to students only because of their desire to cooperate in obtaining data. Furthermore, many cases predated the development of the 0 (Si) scale and the K scale so that these data were not available at the time of the conferences. It would appear that most of the deficiencies in the data do not detract from the positive findings but may have prevented identification of other categories for which the data were too few for statistical analysis.

Information from studies such as these must be used with caution as well as ingenuity. When a particular pattern is found to occur more often in a subgroup than in a total group, it may be helpful in constructing a description of the individual counselee. However, the same pattern may also differentiate other subgroups. For example, the pattern of Scales 7 (Pt) and 8 (Sc) paired high differentiated the male students called tense, but it also occurred more frequently in the subgroups labeled confused, indecisive, vague in goals, lacking in knowledge or information, introverted, and nonresponsive than in the male group as a whole. In studying a profile to form hypotheses about an individual, the problem may well be to determine which description or descriptions are most appropriate.

Sometimes the rest of the profile aids the interpretation; for example, when a low coding of Scale 0 (Si) occurs with 7 and 8 paired high, it lessens the likelihood of the person's being introverted. Beyond this the counselor must consider the possible alternatives, seek any supporting or contrary data, and try out the various hypotheses.

It is also possible from data of this type to build descriptions of patterns, and constructs about a pattern, that go beyond the data. However, it must be remembered that not only does the same pattern differentiate different subgroups, but it may differentiate only a part of any one subgroup. Other patterns also may be related to the same problem or category, or the category itself may be a mixed one, containing different groups that happened to be labeled in the same way by the counselors. The category "wants reassurance only" appears to be of this latter type. It is related to a number of different patterns, but these fall into two groups. One group of patterns suggests that the persons involved were very dependent and were seeking reassurance for this reason. In the other group the counselees were apparently rather well-adjusted persons with well-organized goals, who sought reassurance only to satisfy their curiosity about the results of counseling.

The following summary and discussion of the scales and patterns of scales is not intended to be an accurate statement of statistical findings. It is, rather, an attempt to fit together some constructs and hypotheses about the statistical findings so that ideas may be generated regarding the way the scales operate to form patterns, which in turn may suggest hypotheses for counseling. The generalizations are based on a detailed analysis of the data and on our experience in using the codebook for several years. Others, in using the same data, may come to different conclusions; we have changed our own conclusions about the operation of certain scales many times. The codebook section presents the experimental data with no attempt at interpretation or analysis, but tentative opinions are presented here to help the counselor go beyond a simple consideration of the variables listed in the codebook to what Hathaway has termed a "second level interpretation" of the MMPI profile. While hypotheses based on this level of interpretation must be used very carefully, they are sometimes even more profitable than actuarial data in leading to a better understanding of the individual counselee.

It must always be remembered that interpretations of this type depend greatly on the accuracy of the opinions that go into their formations. One study (5) has demonstrated the possibility of testing these opinions, and further studies of the same nature are planned, but, for the time being, the conclusions we have drawn will have to stand on the interrelationships of the data and the type of clinical intuition that Meehl might call a "multiplicity of concrete experiences."

Scale 0 (Social Introversion-Extroversion)

MEN

This scale was derived and cross-validated (2, 6) as a part of the series of studies on which the present volume is based in order to measure a characteristic which was thought to be important in college adjustment and which did not appear to be measured directly by any of the original scales. It has subsequently been added to the scoring keys and profile sheets distributed by the publisher. Since Scale 0 was derived and cross-validated on a college group, it is not surprising to find that patterns including this scale are related to various aspects of social adjustment in college. Patterns with a high coding of Scale 0 were found among persons showing introvertive characteristics, especially shyness, social insecurity, and social withdrawal. The other scales when combined with Scale 0 often gave an indication of the type and seriousness of the social adjustment problem. For example, when Scale 2 (D) is coded high with Scale 0, the pattern is likely to be associated with a lack of social skills as well as introversion and feelings of social insecurity. When Scale 7 (Pt) is found high with Scale 0, the problem is probably more serious and more extensive. The counselee is likely to be depressed, to be indecisive, and to have a mother conflict. He may also be shy in the interview situation. A high 02 (SiD) coding, then, may be interpreted as indicating a fairly specific problem of shyness or lack of social skills; the high 07 (SiPt) coding indicates a more generalized insecurity in handling social relations. These relations seem to cover a wide range, but may involve particularly the mother and the counselor.

A low coding of Scale 0 is probably indicative of an adequate social adjustment, even in patterns that are usually associated with somewhat serious problems; for example, Scales 29 (DMa) paired high were often indicative of aggressiveness, blocking on examinations, and rationalizing, whereas this pair of scales with Scale 0 coded low was only associated with rationalizing. A more extreme example of the influence of Scale 0 on a pattern is a comparison of Scale 0 coded high along with another

15

scale and Scale 0 coded low with the other scale remaining high. The high pair 05 (SiMf), for example, suggested introversion and shyness, whereas the pattern 5–0 (Scale Mf coded high with Si coded low) was significantly absent among the subgroups of students judged to be tense, nonverbal, introverted, and lacking in skills with the opposite sex. It appears, then, that when Scale 0 is coded low there is a tempering of the problems often associated with the scales making up the rest of the pattern. When coded high the problems appear to center in social adjustment.

WOMEN

The patterns of scales coded high and including Scale 0 differentiated subgroups among the female students similar to those for the men. Any differences that occur appear to be related to sex differences in cultural and social values. In general, Scale 0 coded high is suggestive of social shyness, insecurity, shyness in the interview, and lack of skills with the opposite sex. This latter, lack of skills with the opposite sex, appears particularly when Scale 2 (D) is coded high with Scale 0. It seems likely that the problem resembles that suggested by the 02 (SiD) high coding in men, except that the cultural values of the women may lead to a more specific placement of the problem in the area of relations with men. These female students also tended to lack self-confidence, which might have been due in part to their problems in heterosexual social relations. On the other hand, the problems in heterosexual relations may have been caused by their lack of self-confidence.

When Scale 6 (Pa) is paired high with Scale 0, the problem of the social role of women in our society is again emphasized. This pattern is indicative of feelings of inferiority in regard to some physical feature. Whether the sensitivity to the opinions of others suggested by Scale 6 combined with the social inadequacy suggested by Scale 0 leads to these feelings, or whether the elevation on both scales is a result of the feelings of physical inferiority, cannot be determined from the data. Probably both causation and consequence are involved. When counseling leads to a more realistic assessment of the role of physical attractiveness in heterosexual relations, self-confidence may be developed and personal sensitivity reduced. A realistic assessment is particularly important since a good proportion of the feelings of physical inferiority among counselees do not appear to have an adequate basis in fact but may be the result of stereotypes adopted from advertising and commercial promotion.

16

CONSTRUCTION OF HYPOTHESES

When Scale 7 (Pt) is coded high with Scale 0, it seems to be related to the same type of problems, but probably also to a more generalized feeling of insecurity. Scale 8 (Sc), when coded high with 0, not only suggests shyness but a problem in communicating with the counselor as well. Women with this coding tended to be shy in the interview, unable to talk well to the counselor, and nervous.

When Scale 0 is coded low it appears to indicate a good general adjustment, especially socially, as was found for the male students. There were some differences, however. In women, the ability to adjust socially seems to extend to parental relationships, whereas in the men a low coding of Scale 0 did not suggest freedom from parental conflicts. Furthermore, patterns with a low coding of Scale 0 for the women did not appear to be related to overaggressiveness as was sometimes the case with the men. Such codings indicated that the women were more likely to be marriage oriented and lacking in academic motivation. These differences, again, may reflect the influence of differences in culture and values for the sexes.

Scale 1 (Hypochondriasis)

MEN

Patterns that included a high coding of Scale 1 were relatively infrequent in the college group and were not particularly related to the problems met in counseling. Since Scale 1 was derived from a study of people with vague and generalized physical symptoms (12), it may be that students bothered by the sort of problems associated with an elevation of this scale sought medical aid rather than counseling. It is also possible that the counseling situation did not bring out the attitudes and feelings of the clients in a way that led to their being classified as hypochondriachal. Counselors as a group would tend to refer general complaints to a medical service without attempting to evaluate them.

A low coding of Scale 1 for the male students, on the other hand, tended to support Scales 5 (Mf) and 7 (Pt) coded high in patterns suggesting home conflict. A low Scale 1 also indicated such problems in counseling as nonresponsiveness or poor rapport, particularly when Scale 7 (Pt) was coded high or when the profile was otherwise elevated.

WOMEN

Although elevation of Scale 1 was infrequent among college women, it was related to the physical symptom of headaches when combined with a

17

low coding of Scale 5. There is some evidence here that Scale 1 is operating as an indicator of hypochondriacal symptoms for female counselees, but such symptoms are likely to be rare in the college counseling situation.

Scale 1 coded low may, for the women as for the men, appear to intensify certain problems suggested by the high codings. If a high coding of Scale 1 suggests a tendency to use physical symptoms as a defense, a low coding may suggest infrequent use of this kind of defense and a more frequent occurrence of other kinds of behavior. That is, the client with a low Scale 1 tends to have more generalized symptoms and more of them.

Scale 2 (Depression)

MEN

Scale 2 was derived from the study of a group of patients showing definite symptoms of depression (9). In the selection of items for the scale, a group of normals who were judged to be depressed were also included.

In the present study, as would be expected, patterns with Scale 2 coded high were also indicative of unhappiness or depression. The pattern of the rest of the profile may provide some information about the type of depression and the form it will take. As mentioned in the discussion of Scale 0, the 02 (SiD) high coding suggests a lack of social skills along with the introverted characteristics. Half of the profiles with Scale 0 coded high also had a high coding of Scale 2. This is a further indication of the importance of the social milieu for a satisfactory adjustment. It suggests too that elevation of Scale 2 may be rather strongly related to concern over problems in the area of human relations. Counselees who have problems in adjusting to the academic phases of college life also tend to have an elevation of Scale 2. It was frequently found coded high in patterns suggesting blocking or tension on examinations. In patterns in which Scale 0 (Si) is also coded high, the unhappiness suggested by Scale 2 seems related to a rather specific problem and may be a reflection of dissatisfaction with some aspect of the immediate environment. However, when the whole profile is elevated, and particularly when Scale 7 (Pt) is also coded high, there appears to be a more generalized emotional problem with unhappiness only a part of the syndrome. Such patterns suggest not only depression and introversion, but lack of skills with the opposite sex and deeper anxieties including a great deal of worry, tension, and insomnia.

18

CONSTRUCTION OF HYPOTHESES

WOMEN

In the female group, elevation of Scale 2 seems to reflect not only depression but, more generally, anxiety, lack of self-confidence, and lack of skills with the opposite sex. It appears that acceptance by the opposite sex is more central in the social adjustment of girls than of boys and that uncertainty about this acceptance leads to a more intense depression or anxiety. The anxiety is particularly noticeable when Scale 2 is coded high and Scale 5 is coded low, which suggests that the more feminine girl may attach the most importance to these relationships. There is some evidence, of a rather complex nature, that Scale 2 is primarily an indicator of the affective state of the girl and that identification of the problem leading to that affective state depends on the rest of the profile. For example, some patterns involving Scale 2 are indicators of conflict in the home. When Scale 2 is coded high with Scale 4 (Pd), it suggests father conflict. When this same pair is coded high and Scale 5 (Mf) is coded low, suggesting a more feminine girl, father conflict is not indicated but mother conflict is. On the other hand, when Scale 2 is coded high with Scale 5 (Mf) coded low, neither father nor mother conflict is indicated. Apparently Scale 4 (Pd), in this combination at least, is indicative of the possibility of conflict. Whether the conflict is more likely to occur with the mother or the father is suggested by the presence or absence of Scale 5 (Mf), and the elevation of Scale 2 reflects the resulting affective state.

Another indication of the intensity of the female reaction to social acceptance and success may be found in the patterns with Scale 2 coded low. Of the six patterns with Scale 2 coded low which were differential in this study, five were related to extroversion or socially outgoing characteristics.

Scale 3 (Hysteria)

MEN

The derivation of this scale was based upon patients who apparently had developed physical or psychological illnesses as a solution to problems (13). One of the chief problems in the original validation was the differentiation of the effect of Scale 3 from that of Scale 1 (Hs). From the present studies it appears that the operation of Scale 3 in college students is somewhat different, and no similar difficulty was evident.

Scale 3 coded high with a low coding of Scale 0 (Si) indicates a good general adjustment particularly in social relations but also in verbal skills

19

and in the ability to reason effectively. The same pattern, at times, may also suggest a tendency toward aggressiveness and insistence upon direct answers in counseling. In addition, patterns including this scale coded high were frequently associated with the group of men who failed to carry through with counseling sessions. This failure to continue in counseling might have been due to a disposition of these counselees to be independent or to their ability to resolve their own problems through good verbal skills and effective reasoning. On the other hand, the relation of high codings of Scale 3 to social factors suggests that some of these men were so busy socially that they simply did not take the time to return to counseling. There is evidence that Scale 5 (Mf) coded high operates as a controlling factor in relation to a high coding of Scale 3. This pairing of high 5 and 3 suggests less aggressiveness and more dependence on the part of the counselee. Where part of a profile suggests aggressiveness and a tendency not to return to counseling, and another part of the profile suggests a more dependent attitude and a number of counseling interviews, there is probably some mutual control of these problems. For example, men with a coding of Scale 3 high and Scale 0 (Si) low, but without 5 (Mf) high, tend to be aggressive and fail to return to counseling. Those with 3 and 5 (Mf) paired high tend to be rather dependent and to have a great number of interviews. Profile patterns with both 3 and 5 (Mf) high, and 0 (Si) low, probably tend to form a middle group of some sort. This sort of relationship has been demonstrated in other patterns and, although not yet definitely proved in this one, illustrates the type of considerations that must be taken into account in interpreting patterns in an MMPI profile.

A low coding of Scale 3 did not differentiate any of the subgroups and hence does not appear to be a significant factor at present in the interpretation of MMPI profiles for male counselees.

WOMEN

For women as for men, when this scale is coded high it appears to be indicative of a lack of social problems. However, as was noticed with Scale 1 (Hs), there is evidence that some of the women who have this scale coded high show symptoms related to the original criterion group. The interpretation depends on the low scale associated with the pattern. When Scale 5 (Mf) is coded low some physical complaints, such as headaches and exhaustion, are usually noted. On the other hand, when Scale

0 (Si) is coded low, a more socially outgoing and marriage-oriented girl is suggested.

While the low coding of Scale 0 (Si) with a high coding of Scale 3 is usually indicative of a good general adjustment, there is an exception when Scale 7 (Pt) is also coded high. In this case, there may be a tendency for the girl to lack academic drive, to be anxious, and to have insomnia. Her anxieties, however, are apparently not concerned with social problems, since the same pattern was not related to any of the subgroups having such problems.

Although a few patterns involving Scale 3 coded low are found in female profiles, the interpretation seems to depend on the high coded scales. A low coding of Scale 3 is probably of little importance in interpreting MMPI profiles for female counselees at present.

Scale 4 (Psychopathic Deviate)

MEN

Scale 4 was originally derived from the responses of a group judged to be psychopathic deviates (13). Such persons were often young, had a history of delinquency, and appeared to be uncontrolled by the ordinary mores of society. They also tended to have a fairly high level of intelligence and presented a superficially appealing personality. The resulting halo effect makes it difficult to identify the psychopathic deviate before he gets into trouble, and often causes the counselor to expend a great deal of effort on these cases in spite of their poor prognosis for success. The scale works reasonably well in identifying psychopathic deviates and certain delinquents, especially when Scale 9 (Ma) is also high.

There is little direct evidence of delinquency or psychopathic personality in the present studies. The delinquent appears to be rare in the college population upon which they were based. There may be several reasons for this: the usually low academic motivation of delinquents would lead relatively few to seek a college education; the delinquent is less likely than other students to seek assistance from a service such as a student counseling center; because of the superficially pleasing personality traits of the delinquent, counselors may fail to identify the basic pattern unless other evidence is quite obvious. There is, however, some indirect support of the tendency for this scale to indicate an antagonism to authority when it appears in a male college student's profile. Scale 4, in combination with other scales, often is associated with aggressive behavior, especially when paired high with Scale 9 (Ma), and with Scale 2 (D) coded low. When Scale 4 is coded high with Scale 0 (Si) low, it suggests both aggressiveness and father conflict, and when coded high with Scale 7 (Pt) it suggests home conflicts. There is, then, support for the suggestion that this scale is associated with aggressive, if not belligerent, attitudes toward authority, which may be particularly reflected in the counselee's relations with his father and in the home. On the other hand, a high coding of Scale 4 is not always related to outward indications of aggressiveness. It can be found coded high in patterns associated with behavior indicative of internalized feelings. With high 6 (Pa) it may suggest anxieties, and with a high coding of Scale 7 (Pt), introversion.

Low codings of Scale 4 suggest a need for reassurance in counseling, possibly as a result of concern regarding the attitudes of other people. If this interpretation is correct, a low coding of Scale 4 would seem to be indicative of conformity with the mores of the social group.

WOMEN

In the present study, there is no subgroup of women comparable to the male group described as aggressive or belligerent. Instead, the combination of Scale 4 with Scale 9 (Ma) coded high suggests extroverted or socially outgoing behavior. On the other hand, home conflict is indicated by some of the profiles with Scale 4 coded high, when either Scale 2 (D) or Scale 9 (Ma) is also coded high. It is possible that rebelliousness and aggressiveness is more frequently expressed in this way by women. Scale 5 (Mf) is frequently coded low in college women, and may be functioning as a control of aggressive behavior. Combinations of Scale 4 coded high with Scale 5 (Mf) low suggest anxiety, indecision, and lack of skills with the opposite sex.

Scale 5 (Masculinity-Femininity)

MEN

Scale 5, the Mf scale, was the least well validated of the basic scales on the MMPI (8). It was designed to assist in the identification of homosexuals, but the heterogeneity of the homosexual group, both in ontogeny and in response patterns, prevented an adequate differentiation from normals. Consequently, basing a hypothesis of homosexuality on an elevation of Scale 5 would be very risky.

A high coding of this scale among men is particularly frequent in an educational setting. In spite of, or perhaps because of, the mixed nature of the scale, it is one of the more valuable scales in counseling students. But it is definitely not a simple scale to interpret. The interpretation, even more than usual, depends upon the pattern of the other scales. Conversely, interpretation of some other scales is highly dependent on the existence, or lack, of a high coding of Scale 5. In forming hypotheses, Scale 5 coded high with Scales 4 (Pd), 7 (Pt), 8 (Sc), or 9 (Ma) suggests home conflicts. Either Scale 5 or Scale 7 (Pt) is present in almost all the patterns related to the home conflict group. The hypothesis may be almost completely different when the high coding occurs with Scales 1 (Hs), 2 (D), or 3 (Hy). Scale 5 may support Scale 2 (D) in indicating a tendency to worry or to have insomnia, and may combine with Scales 1 (Hs) and 3 (Hy) to indicate home dependency rather than conflict. With Scale 3 (Hy), in particular, there may also be a tendency to transfer dependency to the counselor with a corresponding increase in the number of counseling interviews. When Scale 2 (D) or 3 (Hy) is coded high with Scale 5 in a profile with no scale coded low, lack of skills with the opposite sex may also be indicated.

In general, when Scale 5 is coded high with members of the so-called neurotic triad, scales 1 (Hs), 2 (D), and 3 (Hy), it suggests a rather dependent person who lacks confidence in himself, but Scale 0 (Si) coded low may modify this interpretation considerably and suggest independence rather than dependence. The pattern of Scale 0 (Si) coded low with high 5 is infrequent among introverted persons or those lacking in skills with the opposite sex. The general relation of Scale 0 (Si) to the more aggressive modes of adjustment supports this suggestion, and the possible operation of a control mechanism in patterns involving Scale 5 high, Scale 3 (Hy) high, and Scale 0 (Si) low has already been mentioned in the discussion of Scale 3 (Hy). That this pattern may be related to a good general environmental adjustment is also indicated by the lack of both Scale 5 coded high and the 3 (Hy) high with 0 (Si) low pattern in the subgroup showing unrealistic or illogical thinking.

There is considerable evidence of the controlling effect of a high coding of Scale 5. Elevation of this scale has previously been suggested (11, pp. 133–134) as a control of what would otherwise be patterns suggestive of delinquency, and, although further investigation is necessary, there is in the present study a strong suggestion of its similar control of aggressive or nonconforming behavior. A high coding of Scale 5 is less frequent in the tense and aggressive subgroups, and among those counselees wanting definite answers or insisting on test scores. The best example, however, is the control exerted by Scale 5 on the pattern indicating lack of academic motivation. In a predictive study (5) of the effect of this pattern on college grades, a high coding of Scale 5 controlled completely the effect of the 89–0 (ScMa–Si) pattern in predicting poor academic work.

In college men, Scale 5 was not coded low frequently enough to be found in any patterns differentiating the subgroups. Instead of a low coding, the lack of a high coding of Scale 5 appears to be the important thing to consider.

In summary, this scale provides a very complex variable in the interpretation of patterns. It may suggest a problem, particularly in relation to home adjustment, or it may control what would otherwise suggest a problem such as aggressive tendencies or a lack of academic motivation.

WOMEN

The data on Scale 5 also appear to be very useful for counseling with women. This is especially true for the low coding of the scale, which is comparable to a high coding for men. A low coding of Scale 5 is very frequent among college women, and, as with a high coding for men, interpretations are complex. In some cases it is a necessary part of a pattern that suggests a hypothesis. In other patterns, it appears to intensify or support hypotheses suggested by the rest of the pattern; and in still others it seems to act as a suppressor of behavior that is suggested by the rest of the pattern. In the present study, of the 25 patterns that included Scale 5 coded low 9 differentiated the anxiety group, 6 the group complaining of headaches, and 7 the group complaining of exhaustion. In the patterns suggesting headaches and anxiety, a low coding of Scale 5 seemed to support or intensify the reaction expected from the high codings associated with the patterns. The patterns suggestive of anxiety primarily involved Scales 2 (D), 7 (Pt), or 8 (Sc) coded high, or combinations of these scales coded high. In patterns indicating headaches, Scales 1 (Hs) or 3 (Hy), both indicative of physical complaints, were generally coded high in the pattern. In the case of patterns suggesting exhaustion, Scale 5 does not merely intensify the expectation from the high coding but appears to be itself a necessary element. These patterns are Scale 5 coded low with combinations involving Scales 3 (Hy), 7 (Pt), and 9 (Ma) coded high. However, when these scales

24

are coded high, and Scale 5 is *not* coded low, they do not indicate exhaustion. Of theoretical interest, in support of the necessity for considering patterns of scales, is the observation that none of these scales coded high, no combination of these scales coded high, nor merely Scale 5 coded low, is related to the exhaustion group. Any study of the individual scales attempting to relate them to this criterion would have been doomed to failure from the start.

Scale 5 coded high is found in patterns suggesting an outgoing mode of social adjustment. When Scales 4 (Pd) or 9 (Ma) are paired high with Scale 5, vague goals are indicated. The relation between Scales 4 (Pd) and 9 (Ma) found here and in previous studies of delinquency suggests that the vague goals may be part of a general problem these girls have in adjusting themselves to the standards expected of women in our culture. The more typical feminine goals either do not appeal to them or have been rejected by them. Scale 5 paired high with Scale 4 (Pd) when Scale 0 (Si) is low also suggests a lack of academic drive.

In summary, it appears that Scale 5 coded low may fit a more or less general concept of femininity, in intensifying some of the behavior associated with other scales. Physical weakness or complaints may be interpreted as reinforcing the dependent self-concept of the female. The high coding of the scale appears to be associated with more socially outgoing behavior, along with vagueness of goals. The frequent low coding of Scale 5 may also account for the relative lack of discrimination of aggressive behavior by Scale 4 (Pd) if it is assumed that Scale 5 acts as a suppressor on the aggressive behavior of women in a similar way to that hypothesized for men.

Scale 6 (Paranoid)

MEN

Scale 6, Pa, was constructed from the study of patients judged to have paranoid reactions including milder symptoms such as interpersonal sensitivity, suspiciousness, and rigidity of opinions and attitudes. The authors state that the scale is weak but in combination with Scale 8 (Sc) is more effective in identifying paranoid schizophrenics than any single scale or pool of items (8).

Only one pattern was found in the present study that included a high coding of Scale 6. When paired high with Scale 4 (Pd), it differentiated the anxiety subgroup. If Scale 6 is related to sensitivity and suspiciousness in normals, it is quite possible that other patterns involving this scale did not differentiate any groups successfully because the counselees were defensive or superficial in the interview situation in order to avoid revealing themselves, and hence their problems did not become evident to the counselor. A low coding of Scale 6 along with a high coding of Scale 9 (Ma) indicated rationalizing in the interview. The low coding of Scale 6 may reflect personal insensitivity, in that these counselees often shift the blame for their own faults to others.

WOMEN

Scale 6, as was found with some other scales, differentiates the college women better than the men and for them indicates more clearly an extension of the meaning of the original validation of the scale. When coded high in certain patterns, it suggested a personal sensitivity about some physical defect, even though at times the defect was not visible to the counselor. When coded high with Scale 8 (Sc), or when coded in a profile which had no scales coded low, Scale 6 also suggested that long-term counseling was necessary. A continuance of counseling sessions may indicate intensity of personal sensitivity as well as some overdependency on the counselor. Scale 6 coded low with Scale 4 (Pd) coded high was associated with vague goals. Scale 6 coded low with Scale 2 coded high suggested lack of confidence. These findings may be dependent wholly on the high codings involved rather than indicate any influence of the low coding of Scale 6.

In summary, it appears that there is support for the interpretation of a high coding of Scale 6 as an indicator of personal sensitivity and perhaps extreme concern about the reactions of others to something perceived by the counselee as a deficiency. A low score may indicate a lack of personal sensitivity to the reactions of others.

Scale 7 (Psychasthenia)
MEN

Scale 7, Pt, was derived from a study of clinical patients exhibiting compulsions, obsessions, phobias, vacillation, excessive worry, and lack of confidence, a mixed group of symptoms generally labeled as psychasthenic (14).

In the present studies, high Scale 7 appears to be related to general anxiety states. Variations in the picture depend on which scale is elevated along with Scale 7. When Scale 2 (D) is paired high with Scale 7, tension and indecisiveness are associated with the worries and anxiety, whereas when Scale 8 (Sc) is the second member of the high pair, confusion and disorganized thinking appear. In either of these patterns, the central problems are much the same but they overlap and spread into other areas as well, such as social adjustment, conflict with the family, and lack of skills with the opposite sex. While Scale 7 coded high is frequently found in profiles of students with serious problems, elevation of this scale is not always associated with serious difficulties. Low coding of Scale 0 (Si) is infrequent among tense, indecisive, and nonresponsive persons, and this scale may modify some of the effects of a high coding of Scale 7. Scales 5 (Mf) and 9 (Ma) coded high may also be a control for the high coding of Scale 7 as it is related to serious personal maladjustment. The same patterns, however, probably do not control the tendency of Scale 7 to indicate home conflict. Home conflict is suggested, in fact, by combinations of Scale 7 coded high with Scales 4 (Pd), 5 (Mf), and 9 (Ma) high.

A low coding of Scale 7 did not occur very frequently either in the total group of men or in any subgroup. When it did occur it appeared to be indicative of rather good adjustment. A low coding alone and in combination with Scale 0 (Si) coded low was associated with the group of counselees who were judged to be seeking some confirmation for decisions already made. About half of the low codings of this scale were paired with a low coding of Scale 0 (Si), which as was noted previously appears to be associated with good social adjustment.

In summary, elevation of Scale 7, particularly with Scales 2 (D) or 8 (Sc) coded high, or in a profile with no scale coded low, may be an indication that long-term counseling is necessary. Men with these patterns may be particularly difficult counseling cases since such profiles also suggest they have difficulty in making decisions. The findings here appear to fit very well the clinical findings for this scale.

WOMEN

This scale yields information for counseling with women similar to that for men except that it appears to be more closely related to feelings of insecurity for the women. The scale combines in quite a few patterns all of which are suggestive of problems requiring therapeutic treatment. The various combinations suggest exhaustion, insomnia, lack of self-confidence, social shyness, and social insecurity. Profiles with this scale coded high and Scale 5 (Mf) coded low resemble the generally elevated profiles of men with no scales coded low. Physical complaints, anxieties, and insecurities were frequently present. The intensifying effect associated with a low coding of Scale 5 (Mf) has been discussed under that scale. Although Scale 0 (Si) coded low appears to control some of the effects of a high coding of Scale 7 in men, it does not occur frequently enough in women to justify a similar suggestion for interpretation of their profiles. Most of the combinations of other scales coded high with Scale 7 have been discussed previously. With Scale 0 (Si) high, social problems are indicated. With Scale 2 (D) high, there are not only social problems but depression and anxieties. With Scale 3 (Hy) high, particularly when Scale 5 (Mf) is coded low, physical complaints, such as headaches, exhaustion, insomnia, and nervousness, are common. Scale 7 coded high, for the women as for the men, is often indicative of rather intense reactions and personal problems in the college student, whereas a low coding does not appear frequently enough for either sex to be helpful in counseling.

Scale 8 (Schizophrenia)

MEN

Scale 8 was derived from a study of the responses of a group of mixed schizophrenics (8). The number of diagnosed schizophrenics identified by the scale in the validating work was relatively low. This may have been due in part to the uncertainty of the diagnosis. The scale is believed to be more indicative of a person's distortion of his world — perceiving things differently from others and often reacting to things in unusual ways (11, p. 18). Scale 8 correlates with Scale 7 (Pt) but, as observed in clinical groups, there is a difference in behavior outcomes.

In the present studies the most characteristic finding regarding patterns containing Scale 8 was that of mental disorganization; the students were described by counselors as confused, vague in goals, lacking in knowledge or information, or lacking in academic motivation. When a high coding of Scale 8 is either combined with Scale 7 (Pt) coded high or found in a generally elevated profile, it is related to the group labeled as having vague goals or being confused. On the other hand, when 8 is found high in patterns involving Scale 3 (Hy) high or Scale 0 (Si) low — both of which are associated with a relatively good general adjust-

28

ment — the pattern points to the probably less serious problem of lack of knowledge or information. As indicated above, Scale 8 is often indicative of disorganized thinking, but a low coding of Scale 0 (Si) appears to have some controlling effect; in the construct validation of the academic motivation pattern a high coding of Scale 5 (Mf) in combination with high 8 and low 0 led to a higher distribution of grades (5).

Scale 8, in general, appears to be associated with many of the characteristics of Scale 7 (Pt) except that there are more indications of disorganized thinking or confusion. It was not found to differentiate any subgroups when coded low.

WOMEN

High scale 8 in women appears to indicate a more serious general disturbance than it does in men. Patterns involving Scale 8 seem more serious than those for Scale 7 (Pt), and the high coding of Scale 8 seems to emphasize the characteristics associated with the other scales in the pattern. When Scale 0 (Si) is coded high with Scale 8, nervousness and nonverbal behavior in the interview are indicated as well as introverted characteristics. When the pattern includes Scale 2 (D) coded high with 8, not only is depression indicated, but also deeper anxieties, study problems, and lack of skills with the opposite sex. When Scale 9 (Ma) is combined with 8 coded high, the counselee may be confused, restless, verbal, and resistant in counseling, and may require long-term counseling.

Scale 0 (Si) coded low may control some of the effects of a high coding of Scale 8 for women as it did for men. When Scale 0 (Si) is coded low with 8 high, the only group differentiated was that labeled verbal. On the other hand, when Scale 8 is coded high with no scale coded low, the problems suggested include father, mother, and sibling conflicts, study problems, depression, and lack of skills with the opposite sex.

The high coding of Scale 8 in women suggests problems somewhat characteristic of a high coding of Scale 7 (Pt) in men, and may be roughly comparable in interpretation. As with the men, a low coding of Scale 8 did not differentiate any of the female subgroups.

Scale 9 (Hypomania)

MEN

Scale 9 was derived from a study of a group of persons showing manic excitement as a chief symptom (13). Extreme cases were not used in the study because such patients were unable to cooperate sufficiently in sorting the cards. The criterion group included persons described as being unstable in mood, evidencing excitement, and exhibiting flights of ideas. Hathaway and McKinley (13) report that the scale is useful in the clinical setting especially in the prognosis of outcomes when dealing with delinquents. They consider a high score on the scale to be indicative of ebullient enthusiasm in normals. There is some agreement with this in the findings of the present studies.

In the pattern with Scale 9 coded high and Scale 0 (Si) coded low there was a strong indication of outgoing, verbal, and socially skilled behavior. Other patterns including this scale, but without Scale 0 (Si) coded high, were associated with aggressive behavior. When Scale 0 (Si) was paired high with Scale 9 it appeared to dominate in that the socially shy or withdrawn group was differentiated. Various patterns including Scale 9 indicated conflict in the family situation. The high pair 95 (MaMf) was associated with mother conflict and the high pair 97 (MaPt) with family conflict in general. In some cases Scale 9 appeared to be negatively correlated with Scale 0 (Si) except that Scale 9 high was more suggestive of aggressiveness than Scale 0 (Si) coded low.

Low codings of Scale 9 were found in cases of students wanting reassurance or judged to be rather dependent. This may be interpreted as an indication of lack of drive or lack of independence or lack of ability to express such a drive. It may be that Scale 9 facilitates the expression of behavior associated with some scales, such as Scale 4 (Pd), when it is high and when it is coded low indicates that the behavior usually associated with other scales coded high is not overtly exhibited.

WOMEN

This scale coded high with other scales and especially with Scale 0 (Si) coded low was associated with socially outgoing and verbal behavior in the female students. When Scale 0 (Si) was coded high the results were reversed, as was noted for the men, in that the socially shy group was differentiated. Various combinations of Scale 9 high with other scales high and with Scale 5 (Mf) coded low differentiated the physical exhaustion group. This might be interpreted as indicating a rather extreme feminine reaction to hyperactivity. The group of girls distinguished by the most pattern containing Scale 9 was the group judged to be socially extroverted. On the other hand there was no subgroup of girls of sufficient size comparable to the subgroup for men judged to be aggressive and/or belligerent. It appears, then, that energetic action, usually assumed to be revealed by this scale, is expressed by the girls in more socially approved ways than the men's aggressiveness or belligerence.

Low codings of Scale 9 for the women were usually indicative of social shyness when either Scale 0 (Si) or Scale 2 (D) was coded high.

The Validity Scales: ?, L, F, and K

The first four scales on the usual MMPI profile sheet are called the validity scales and are mainly concerned with the accuracy and reliability of the subjects' responses to the inventory. They were not included for analysis in the studies on which this volume is based, but they were used to discard certain profiles before the studies were begun.

The ? score is the number of items that the subject did not answer on the group form, or the number of items placed in the "Cannot Say" category on the card form of the MMPI. If this score is too high, conclusions based on the profile are not considered valid; profiles on which the ? scale had a T-score of 70 or above were discarded from the present studies. In the practical counseling situation, in spite of all precautions, a profile with a T-score above 70 is occasionally encountered. When this occurs, the counselor may find it more useful to make a cautious interpretation of the profile than simply to eliminate it from consideration. Such profiles are routinely coded at Wisconsin and tentative hypotheses formulated even though the scales may not deviate as much from the mean as they might if more of the items had been answered. It has been observed that an exploration of the attitudes responsible for the large number of unanswered or "Cannot Say" items may be profitable. While interpretations of this sort must be treated with great care, they seem to be reasonably useful.

The L score is based on answers to a group of items that tend to place the test subject in a good social and moral light. High scores on this scale are not common among college subjects, probably because the items are rather naive and concern attitudes that are not felt to be particularly socially rewarding in the college culture. In fact, personal observation suggests that a high L score may be a good indicator of some defensiveness combined with considerable naiveté. A very high L score, that is, a T-score above 70, suggests that some of the results of such a profile analysis should be questioned, particularly those that indicate a strong social development, but does not seem to argue against a careful interpretation of the profile. The question "What is the counselee trying to conceal on the test?" might be asked.

A high F score, that is, T-score above 80, on the other hand, suggests that the person is placing himself in a rather poorer light than an objective view would warrant. The hypothesis that he has faked the profile to look bad would be very rarely borne out in a counseling setting. More likely, a moderate F score indicates one of two things. F tends to be high in some cases where there is a serious problem of personal adjustment. It may also be high where the MMPI is administered after counseling has begun and the counselee feels that the test is giving him an opportunity to reveal his problems to the counselor. In these cases, the profile pattern is likely to suggest reasonably accurate hypotheses in spite of some possible exaggeration due to the test-taking attitude. A high F score may also be an indication of inaccuracy or random responses on the part of the subject, or may identify an error in recording or scoring of the test. As a standard procedure, the psychometrist should recheck the sorting, recording, and scoring of any answer sheet with a high F score, particularly when the card form has been used. Because of the possibility of this kind of error, profiles with an F score of above T-score 80 were discarded from the present study, even though discarding these profiles may also have meant eliminating some of the more serious cases from the criterion groups. While a high F score may also indicate an inability to understand the items on the test, this would be very unusual in most counseling situations. In a series of Minnesota studies, no difficulty was encountered in the testing of thousands of ninth-grade students (11).

The K scale was designed to improve the predictive validity of some of the original scales (15, 17) and is used as a correction on five of them. Partly because its effect is measured to some extent in these scales, the K scale itself was not included in the profile analysis leading to the present volume. K has been considered at times as a rather subtle indicator of defensiveness, and its theoretical basis as a correction scale would support this conclusion to a certain extent. The evidence for this has been rather sketchy, however, and a high K score may have a considerably different meaning. In the college group, at least, a slight elevation of K is very common and may even be a relatively good sign of general adjustment. More complete treatment of interpretation of K will have to await further research on its effect in the interpretation of patterns.

CONSTRUCTION OF HYPOTHESES

In general, the validity scales provide highly useful devices in the forming of hypotheses about the test-taking attitude of the counselee. When they are extreme, and suggest an attitude that might lead to invalidity of the test, the profile may still give some information to the counselor; but it must be interpreted with due regard to the heightened uncertainty of the analysis. Moderate elevations probably do not change the interpretation of the rest of the profile particularly but may add some hypotheses to those suggested by the rest of the profile. Even when a profile is judged to be invalid, the attitude leading to the invalidity may be suggested by these scales and valuable hypotheses may be drawn therefrom.

Codebook of MMPI Patterns

INTRODUCTION TO THE CODEBOOK

The following codebook was designed to help counselors develop hypotheses from MMPI patterns. It is divided into two sections, one for men and the other for women. All patterns of 3 high coded scales with one or no low coded scales are included if any part of the pattern was associated with any of the categories studied.

The first step in using the codebook for a particular profile is to code that profile. This is done by assigning numbers to the scales:

Si	Hs	D	Hy	Pd	Mf	Pa	Pt	Sc	Ma	None
0	1	2	3	4	5	6	7	8	9	X

No scale is coded high unless it has a T-score of 55 or above and no scale is coded low unless it has a T-score of 45 or less. Only the three highest scales are selected to represent the high coding of the profile; that is, if the profile has 5 scales with T-scores above 54 only the 3 highest of the 5 are used in the coded profile. In the case of the low scales only the 2 lowest with T-scores below 46 are coded. After the 3 highest and the two lowest scales are selected, the numbers of the scales are arranged in numerical order regardless of the relative size of the T-scores; a dash (−) separates the numbers for the high scales from the numbers for the low scales. For example, suppose the T-scores for the various scales in a female profile were as follows: Si = 46; Hs = 44; D = 70; Hy = 53; Pd = 45; Mf = 43; Pa = 57; Pt = 69; Sc = 58; Ma = 50. The high scales are D, Pa, Pt, and Sc, but D, Pt, and Sc are the three highest. Substitute the code numbers for the scales to obtain the high code 278. The low scales are Hs, Mf, and Pd, but Hs and Mf are the two lowest. Substitute the code numbers for these scales to obtain the low code 51. These are then combined as follows: 278–15. The profile is now in a form that can be easily found in the codebook. When there are, as here, two scales coded low, it will be necessary to look in two places in the codebook for the information (in this case under 278–1 and 278–5), but the two entries will always be near each other since the order in the codebook is determined by the high coding. The various hypotheses to be considered in interpreting this profile will be found on page 104 below. If there had been no low coding for this profile, the code number would have been 278–X; see page 105.

Since some profiles were found to have only one or two scales coded high, the codebook also lists hypotheses that may apply to them. Whenever different parts of the profile are associated with types of behavior that appear to be inconsistent, the part of the coding associated with the behavior is indicated by numbers in parentheses immediately following the descriptive terms.

Occasionally there is no listing of a code pattern. In these cases, either the pattern did not occur frequently enough or it was not significantly related to any of the criterion groups. Interpretation of such profiles will have to depend upon the counselor's knowledge of the meanings of the scales and the ways in which they may be interrelated. The discussion of the individual scales in the earlier section of this book may be of some assistance here.

In order to save space, if the description of a pattern of high scales is apparently not affected by certain low coded scales, the low scales are listed together, separated by a slant line. For example, the pattern 012 differentiated the same male subgroups regardless of the low coding; hence this is designated in the codebook as 012–3/4/5/6/7/8/9 and there is only one listing of the descriptive categories applicable to each of these patterns.

One other explanation is necessary for proper interpretation of the descriptions of the code patterns. The description is sometimes followed with a notation that the pattern or some part of it was infrequently associated with certain subgroups. This means that it was significantly absent according to the statistical criterion used. For example, the male code pattern 234–0 reads as follows: "Father conflict, one interview only, aggressive or belligerent, wants answers or insists on test scores. This pattern was infrequently associated with introversion . . ." That is, the pattern was significantly absent. Whether it would have been significantly present in a group judged to be extroverted is not known because such

INTRODUCTION

a group was not large enough to include in the analyses. One might hypothesize that this pattern indicates extroversion but the hypothesis would be weaker than the hypothesis that the pattern indicates lack of introversion.

Tables of data from which the descriptions were derived will be found in the appendix.

0–1/9	Introverted or self-conscious or socially insecure.
01–9	Introverted or self-conscious or socially insecure.
012–3/4/5/6/ 7/8/9	Introverted or self-conscious or socially insecure, lacks social skills.
012–X	Introverted or self-conscious or socially insecure, lacks social skills, lacks skills with the opposite sex, unhappy, worries a great deal, insomnia.
013–9	Introverted or self-conscious or socially insecure.
014–9	Introverted or self-conscious or socially insecure.
015–2/3	Introverted or self-conscious or socially insecure, shy in the interview, home dependency.
015–4	Introverted or self-conscious or socially insecure, shy in the interview, home dependency, home conflict.
015–6/7/8/9	Introverted or self-conscious or socially insecure, shy in the interview, home dependency.
015–X	Introverted or self-conscious or socially insecure, shy in the interview, home dependency, home conflict, insomnia.
016–9	Introverted or self-conscious or socially insecure.
017–2/3/4/5/ 6/8/9	Introverted or self-conscious or socially insecure, shy in the interview, mother conflict, indecisive, unhappy (07).
017–X	Introverted or self-conscious or socially insecure, shy in the interview, lacks skills with the opposite sex, mother conflict, sibling conflict, non-responsive or nonverbal, tense, indecisive, unhappy, worries a great deal, insomnia, confused.
018–9	Introverted or self-conscious or socially insecure.
018–X	Indecisive, unhappy, worries a great deal, insomnia, confused.
019–6	Rationalizes a great deal.
02–1/3/4/5/ 6/7/8/9	Introverted or self-conscious or socially insecure, lacks social skills.
02–X	Introverted or self-conscious or socially insecure, lacks social skills, lacks skills with the opposite sex, tense, unhappy, worries a great deal, insomnia.
023–1/4/5/6/ 7/8/9	Introverted or self-conscious or socially insecure, lacks social skills.
023–X	Introverted or self-conscious or socially insecure, lacks social skills, lacks skills with the opposite sex, tense, unhappy, worries a great deal, insomnia.

MALE SECTION

024–1/3/5/6/ 7/8/9   Introverted or self-conscious or socially insecure, lacks social skills.

024–X   Introverted or self-conscious or socially insecure, lacks social skills, lacks skills with the opposite sex, tense, unhappy, worries a great deal, insomnia. Note: Scale 4 coded high was infrequently associated with lack of skills with the opposite sex.

025–1   Introverted or self-conscious or socially insecure, shy in the interview, lacks social skills, wants reassurance only, restless, worries a great deal.

025–3/4/6/7/ 8/9   Introverted or self-conscious or socially insecure, shy in the interview, lacks social skills, wants reassurance only, worries a great deal.

025–X   Introverted or self-conscious or socially insecure, shy in the interview, lacks social skills, lacks skills with the opposite sex, home conflict, wants reassurance only, tense, unhappy, worries a great deal, insomnia. Note: Scale 5 coded high was infrequently associated with tension.

026–1/3/4/5/ 7/8/9   Introverted or self-conscious or socially insecure, lacks social skills.

026–X   Introverted or self-conscious or socially insecure, lacks social skills, lacks skills with the opposite sex, tense, unhappy, worries a great deal, insomnia.

027–1   Introverted or self-conscious or socially insecure, shy in the interview, lacks social skills, mother conflict, nonresponsive or nonverbal, tense, tense on examinations, indecisive, unhappy, worries a great deal, confused, home conflict.

027–3/4/5/6/ 8   Introverted or self-conscious or socially insecure, shy in the interview, lacks social skills, mother conflict, tense, tense on examinations, indecisive, unhappy, worries a great deal.

027–9   Introverted or self-conscious or socially insecure, shy in the interview, lacks social skills, mother conflict, generally dependent, tense, tense on examinations, indecisive, unhappy, worries a great deal.

027–X   Introverted or self-conscious or socially insecure, shy in the interview, lacks social skills, lacks skills with the opposite sex, home conflict, mother conflict, sibling conflict, nonresponsive or nonverbal, tense, tense on examinations, indecisive, unhappy, worries a great deal, insomnia, confused.

028–1/3/4/5/ 6/7/9   Introverted or self-conscious or socially insecure, lacks social skills, lacks skills with the opposite sex.

028–X   Introverted or self-conscious or socially insecure, lacks social skills, lacks skills with the opposite sex, tense, indecisive, unhappy, worries a great deal, insomnia, confused.

029–1/3/4/5/ 6/7/8   Introverted or self-conscious or socially insecure, lacks social skills, tense on examinations, aggressive or belligerent, rationalizes a great deal.

029–X   Introverted or self-conscious or socially insecure, lacks social skills, lacks skills with the opposite sex, tense, tense on examinations, unhappy, worries a great deal, insomnia, aggressive or belligerent, rationalizes a great deal. Note: Scale 9 coded high was infrequently associated with lack of skills with the opposite sex and worrying a great deal.

03–1/9   Introverted or self-conscious or socially insecure.

034–1/9   Introverted or self-conscious or socially insecure.

CODEBOOK OF MMPI PATTERNS

035–1
Introverted or self-conscious or socially insecure, shy in the interview, home dependency, four or more conferences, restless. Note: Scale 3 coded high was infrequently associated with restlessness.

035–2/4/6/7/
8/9
Introverted or self-conscious or socially insecure, shy in the interview, home dependency, four or more conferences.

035–X
Introverted or self-conscious or socially insecure, shy in the interview, lacks skills with the opposite sex, home dependency, home conflict, four or more conferences, insomnia.

036–1/9
Introverted or self-conscious or socially insecure.

037–1
Introverted or self-conscious or socially insecure, shy in the interview, mother conflict, nonresponsive or nonverbal, indecisive, unhappy. Note: Scale 3 coded high was infrequently associated with mother conflict.

037–2/4/5/6/
8/9
Introverted or self-conscious or socially insecure, shy in the interview, mother conflict, indecisive, unhappy (07). Note: Scale 3 coded high was infrequently associated with mother conflict.

037–X
Introverted or self-conscious or socially insecure, shy in the interview, lacks skills with the opposite sex, mother conflict, sibling conflict, nonresponsive or nonverbal, tense, indecisive, unhappy, worries a great deal, insomnia, confused. Note: Scale 3 coded high was infrequently associated with mother conflict.

038–1
Introverted or self-conscious or socially insecure, lacks knowledge or information.

038–2/4/5/6/
7
Lacks knowledge or information.

038–9
Introverted or self-conscious or socially insecure, lacks knowledge or information.

038–X
Indecisive, unhappy, worries a great deal, insomnia, lacks knowledge or information, confused.

039–1
Introverted or self-conscious or socially insecure.

039–6
Rationalizes a great deal.

04–1/9
Introverted or self-conscious or socially insecure.

045–1
Introverted or self-conscious or socially insecure, shy in the interview, home conflict, restless.

045–2/3/6/7/
8/9
Introverted or self-conscious or socially insecure, shy in the interview.

045–X
Introverted or self-conscious or socially insecure, shy in the interview, home conflict, insomnia.

046–1
Introverted or self-conscious or socially insecure, worries a great deal.

046–2/3/5/7/
8
Worries a great deal.

046–9
Introverted or self-conscious or socially insecure, worries a great deal.

047–1
Introverted or self-conscious or socially insecure, shy in the interview, home conflict, mother conflict, indecisive, unhappy, nonresponsive or nonverbal.

047–2/3/5/6
8/9
Introverted or self-conscious or socially insecure, shy in the interview, home conflict, mother conflict, indecisive, unhappy (07).

047–X
Introverted or self-conscious or socially insecure, shy in the interview, lacks skills with the opposite sex, home conflict, mother conflict, sibling conflict, indecisive, tense, unhappy, worries a great deal, insomnia, con-

fused, nonresponsive or nonverbal, poor rapport. Note: Scale 4 coded high was infrequently associated with lack of skills with the opposite sex.

048–1/9	Introverted or self-conscious or socially insecure.
048–X	Indecisive, unhappy, worries a great deal, insomnia, confused.
049–1	Introverted or self-conscious or socially insecure.
049–2	Aggressive or belligerent.
049–6	Rationalizes a great deal.
05–1	Introverted or self-conscious or socially insecure, shy in the interview, restless.
05–2/3/4/6/ 7/8/9	Introverted or self-conscious or socially insecure, shy in the interview.
05–X	Introverted or self-conscious or socially insecure, shy in the interview, home conflict, insomnia.
056–1	Introverted or self-conscious or socially insecure, shy in the interview, restless.
056–2/3/4/7/ 8/9	Introverted or self-conscious or socially insecure, shy in the interview.
056–X	Introverted or self-conscious or socially insecure, shy in the interview, home conflict, insomnia.
057–1	Introverted or self-conscious or socially insecure, shy in the interview, home conflict, mother conflict, wants reassurance only, nonresponsive or nonverbal, indecisive, restless, unhappy.
057–2/3/4/6/ 8/9	Introverted or self-conscious or socially insecure, shy in the interview, home conflict, mother conflict, wants reassurance only, indecisive, unhappy (07).
057–X	Introverted or self-conscious or socially insecure, shy in the interview, lacks skills with the opposite sex, home conflict, mother conflict, sibling conflict, wants reassurance only, nonresponsive or nonverbal, tense, indecisive, unhappy, worries a great deal, insomnia, confused. Note: Scale 5 coded high was infrequently associated with tension.
058–1	Introverted or self-conscious or socially insecure, shy in the interview, home conflict, restless.
058–2/3/4/6/ 7/9	Introverted or self-conscious or socially insecure, shy in the interview, home conflict.
058–X	Introverted or self-conscious or socially insecure, shy in the interview, home conflict, indecisive, unhappy, worries a great deal, insomnia, confused.
059–1	Introverted or self-conscious or socially insecure, shy in the interview, mother conflict, poor rapport, restless.
059–2/3/4	Introverted or self-conscious or socially insecure, shy in the interview, mother conflict, poor rapport.
059–6	Introverted or self-conscious or socially insecure, shy in the interview, mother conflict, poor rapport, rationalizes a great deal.
059–7/8	Introverted or self-conscious or socially insecure, shy in the interview, mother conflict, poor rapport.
059–X	Introverted or self-conscious or socially insecure, shy in the interview, home conflict, mother conflict, poor rapport, insomnia.
06–1/9	Introverted or self-conscious or socially insecure.

067–1   Introverted or self-conscious or socially insecure, shy in the interview, mother conflict, indecisive, unhappy, nonresponsive or nonverbal.

067–2/3/4/5/   Introverted or self-conscious or socially insecure, shy in the interview, mother conflict, indecisive, unhappy (07).
8/9

067–X   Introverted or self-conscious or socially insecure, shy in the interview, lacks skills with the opposite sex, mother conflict, sibling conflict, indecisive, tense, unhappy, worries a great deal, insomnia, confused, nonresponsive or nonverbal.

068–1/9   Introverted or self-conscious or socially insecure.

068–X   Indecisive, unhappy, worries a great deal, insomnia, confused.

069–1   Introverted or self-conscious or socially insecure.

07–1   Introverted or self-conscious or socially insecure, shy in the interview, mother conflict, indecisive, unhappy, nonresponsive or nonverbal, home conflict.

07–2/3/4/5/   Introverted or self-conscious or socially insecure, shy in the interview, mother conflict, indecisive, unhappy (07).
6/8/9

07–X   Introverted or self-conscious or socially insecure, shy in the interview, lacks skills with the opposite sex, mother conflict, sibling conflict, indecisive, tense, unhappy, worries a great deal, insomnia, confused, nonresponsive or nonverbal.

078–1/2/3/4/   Introverted or self-conscious or socially insecure, shy in the interview, mother conflict, nonresponsive or nonverbal, tense, indecisive, unhappy
5/6/9   (07), lacking in knowledge or information, vague goals, confused.

078–X   Introverted or self-conscious or socially insecure, shy in the interview, lacks skills with the opposite sex, mother conflict, sibling conflict, nonresponsive or nonverbal, tense, indecisive, unhappy, lacks knowledge or information, vague goals, confused, worries a great deal, insomnia.

079–1   Introverted or self-conscious or socially insecure, shy in the interview, home conflict, mother conflict, nonresponsive or nonverbal, indecisive, unhappy, defensive. Note: Scale 9 coded high was infrequently associated with being nonresponsive or nonverbal and with indecisiveness.

079–2/3/4/5   Introverted or self-conscious or socially insecure, shy in the interview, home conflict, mother conflict, indecisive, unhappy (07), defensive. Note: Scale 9 coded high was infrequently associated with indecisiveness.

079–6   Introverted or self-conscious or socially insecure, shy in the interview, home conflict, mother conflict, indecisive, unhappy, defensive, rationalizes a great deal. Note: Scale 9 coded high was infrequently associated with indecisiveness.

079–8   Introverted or self-conscious or socially insecure, shy in the interview, home conflict, mother conflict, unhappy, defensive, indecisive. Note: Scale 9 coded high was infrequently associated with indecisiveness.

079–X   Introverted or self-conscious or socially insecure, shy in the interview, lacks skills with the opposite sex, home conflict, mother conflict, sibling conflict, nonresponsive or nonverbal, tense, indecisive, unhappy, worries a great deal, insomnia, confused, defensive. Note: Scale 9 coded high was infrequently associated with lack of skills with the opposite sex, being nonresponsive or nonverbal, indecisiveness, worrying a great deal.

08–1/9   Introverted or self-conscious or socially insecure.

MALE SECTION

08–X	Indecisive, unhappy, worries a great deal, insomnia, confused.
089–1	Introverted or self-conscious or socially insecure.
089–6	Rationalizes a great deal.
089–X	Indecisive, unhappy, worries a great deal, confused, insomnia. Note: Scale 9 coded high was infrequently associated with indecisiveness and worrying a great deal.
09–1	Introverted or self-conscious or socially insecure.
09–6	Rationalizes a great deal.
123–0	One interview only, aggressive or belligerent, wants answers or insists on test scores. This pattern was infrequently associated with introversion or self-consciousness or social insecurity, lack of social skills, mother conflict, being nonresponsive or nonverbal, being nonverbal or a non-relator, being unrealistic or illogical, restlessness, unhappiness.
123–X	Introverted or self-conscious or socially insecure, lacks skills with the opposite sex, tense, unhappy, worries a great deal, insomnia.
124–0	Father conflict, aggressive or belligerent.
124–X	Introverted or self-conscious or socially insecure, lacks skills with the opposite sex, tense, unhappy, worries a great deal, insomnia. Note: Scale 4 coded high was infrequently associated with lack of skills with the opposite sex.
125–0	Home dependency, worries a great deal, wants reassurance only. Note: Scale 0 coded low was infrequently associated with worrying a great deal. This pattern was infrequently associated with introversion or self-consciousness or social insecurity, being nonresponsive or nonverbal, tension.
125–3	Home dependency, wants reassurance only, worries a great deal.
125–4	Home dependency, home conflict, wants reassurance only, worries a great deal.
125–6/7/8/9	Home dependency, wants reassurance only, worries a great deal.
125–X	Introverted or self-conscious or socially insecure, lacks skills with the opposite sex, home conflict, home dependency, wants reassurance only, tense, unhappy, worries a great deal, insomnia. Note: Scale 5 coded high was infrequently associated with tension.
126–X	Introverted or self-conscious or socially insecure, lacks skills with the opposite sex, tense, unhappy, worries a great deal, insomnia.
127–0	One interview only, tense, tense on examinations, indecisive, unhappy, worries a great deal, lacks knowledge or information. Note: Scale 0 coded low was infrequently associated with indecisiveness, unhappiness, worrying a great deal.
127–3/4/5/6/8	Tense, tense on examinations, indecisive, unhappy, worries a great deal.
127–9	Tense, tense on examinations, indecisive, unhappy, worries a great deal, generally dependent.
127–X	Introverted or self-conscious or socially insecure, lacks social skills, lacks skills with the opposite sex, home conflict, mother conflict, sibling conflict, nonresponsive or nonverbal, tense, tense on examinations, indecisive, unhappy, worries a great deal, insomnia, confused.
128–0	Introverted or self-conscious or socially insecure (28), lacks skills with the opposite sex, lacks knowledge or information, aggressive or belliger-

ent. Note: Scale 0 coded low was infrequently associated with lack of skills with the opposite sex, introversion or self-consciousness or social insecurity.

128–3/4/5/6/7 Introverted or self-conscious or socially insecure, lacks skills with the opposite sex.

128–9 Introverted or self-conscious or socially insecure, lacks skills with the opposite sex.

128–X Introverted or self-conscious or socially insecure, lacks skills with the opposite sex, tense, indecisive, unhappy, worries a great deal, insomnia, confused.

129–0 Tense on examinations, aggressive or belligerent, rationalizes a great deal. This pattern was infrequently associated with introversion or self-consciousness or social insecurity, shyness in the interview, being non-responsive or nonverbal, being nonverbal or a nonrelator, indecisiveness.

129–3/4/5/6/7/8 Tense on examinations, aggressive or belligerent, rationalizes a great deal.

129–X Introverted or self-conscious or socially insecure, lacks skills with the opposite sex, tense, tense on examinations, unhappy, worries a great deal, insomnia, aggressive or belligerent, rationalizes a great deal. Note: Scale 9 coded high was infrequently associated with lack of skills with the opposite sex and worrying a great deal.

13–0 One interview only, aggressive or belligerent, wants answers or insists on test scores. This pattern was infrequently associated with introversion or self-consciousness or social insecurity, lack of social skills, mother conflict, being nonresponsive or nonverbal, being nonverbal or a non-relator, being unrealistic or illogical, nervousness, restlessness, unhappiness.

134–0 Father conflict, one interview only, aggressive or belligerent, wants answers or insists on test scores. This pattern was infrequently associated with introversion or self-consciousness or social insecurity, lack of social skills, mother conflict, being nonresponsive or nonverbal, being nonverbal or a nonrelator, being unrealistic or illogical, nervousness, restlessness, unhappiness.

135–0 Home dependency, four or more conferences (35), one interview only (3–0), aggressive or belligerent, wants answers or insists on test scores. Note: Scale 5 coded high was infrequently associated with wanting answers or insisting on test scores. This pattern was infrequently associated with introversion or self-consciousness or social insecurity, lack of social skills, lack of skills with the opposite sex, mother conflict, being nonresponsive or nonverbal, being nonverbal or a nonrelator, being unrealistic or illogical, nervousness, restlessness, tension, unhappiness.

135–2 Four or more conferences, home dependency.

135–4 Four or more conferences, home dependency, home conflict.

135–6/7/8/9 Four or more conferences, home dependency.

135–X Lacks skills with the opposite sex, home conflict, home dependency, four or more conferences, insomnia.

136–0 One interview only, aggressive or belligerent, wants answers or insists on test scores. This pattern was infrequently associated with introversion or self-consciousness or social insecurity, lack of social skills, mother conflict, being nonresponsive or nonverbal, being nonverbal or a nonrelator, being unrealistic or illogical, nervousness, restlessness, unhappiness.

137–0   One interview only, lacks knowledge or information, aggressive or belligerent, wants answers or insists on test scores. This pattern was infrequently associated with introversion or self-consciousness or social insecurity, lack of social skills, mother conflict, being nonresponsive or nonverbal, being nonverbal or a nonrelator, being unrealistic or illogical, nervousness, restlessness, unhappiness.

137–X   Lacks skills with the opposite sex, mother conflict, sibling conflict, nonresponsive or nonverbal, tense, indecisive, unhappy, worries a great deal, insomnia, confused. Note: Scale 3 coded high was infrequently associated with mother conflict.

138–0   One interview only, lacks knowledge or information, aggressive or belligerent, wants answers or insists on test scores. This pattern was infrequently associated with introversion or self-consciousness or social insecurity, lack of social skills, mother conflict, being nonresponsive or nonverbal, being nonverbal or a nonrelator, being unrealistic or illogical, nervousness, restlessness, unhappiness.

138–2/4/5/6/7   Lacks knowledge or information.

138–9   Introverted or self-conscious or socially insecure, lacks knowledge or information.

138–X   Indecisive, unhappy, worries a great deal, insomnia, lacks knowledge or information, confused.

139–0   One interview only, aggressive or belligerent, wants answers or insists on test scores. This pattern was infrequently associated with introversion or self-consciousness or social insecurity, shyness in the interview, lack of social skills, mother conflict, being nonresponsive or nonverbal, being nonverbal or a nonrelator, being unrealistic or illogical, nervousness, restlessness, indecisiveness, unhappiness.

139–6   Rationalizes a great deal.

14–0   Father conflict, aggressive or belligerent.

145–0   Father conflict, home dependency, aggressive or belligerent. This pattern was infrequently associated with introversion or self-consciousness or social insecurity, lack of skills with the opposite sex, being nonresponsive or nonverbal, tension.

145–2/3/6/7/8/9   Home dependency.

145–X   Home conflict, home dependency, insomnia.

146–0   Father conflict, worries a great deal, aggressive or belligerent. Note: Scale 0 coded low was infrequently associated with worrying a great deal.

146–2/3/5/7/8/9/X   Worries a great deal.

147–0   Home conflict, father conflict, one interview only, lacks knowledge or information, aggressive or belligerent.

147–2/3/5/6/8/9   Home conflict.

147–X   Lacks skills with the opposite sex, home conflict, mother conflict, sibling conflict, nonresponsive or nonverbal, tense, indecisive, unhappy, worries a great deal, insomnia, confused, poor rapport. Note: Scale 4 coded high was infrequently associated with lack of skills with the opposite sex.

148–0	Father conflict, lacks knowledge or information, aggressive or belligerent.
148–9	Introverted or self-conscious or socially insecure.
148–X	Indecisive, unhappy, worries a great deal, insomnia, confused.
149–0	Father conflict, aggressive or belligerent. This pattern was infrequently associated with introversion or self-consciousness or social insecurity, shyness in the interview, being nonresponsive or nonverbal, being nonverbal or a nonrelator, indecisiveness.
149–2	Aggressive or belligerent.
149–6	Rationalizes a great deal.
15–0	Home dependency. This pattern was infrequently associated with introversion or self-consciousness or social insecurity, lack of skills with the opposite sex, being nonresponsive or nonverbal, tension.
15–2/3	Home dependency.
15–4	Home dependency, home conflict.
15–6/7/8/9	Home dependency.
15–X	Home dependency, home conflict, insomnia.
156–0	Home dependency. This pattern was infrequently associated with introversion or self-consciousness or social insecurity, lack of skills with the opposite sex, being nonresponsive or nonverbal, tension.
156–2/3	Home dependency.
156–4	Home dependency, home conflict.
156–7/8/9	Home dependency.
156–X	Home dependency, home conflict, insomnia.
157–0	Home conflict, home dependency, one interview only, wants reassurance only, lacks knowledge or information. This pattern was infrequently associated with introversion or self-consciousness or social insecurity, lack of skills with the opposite sex, being nonresponsive or nonverbal, tension.
157–2/3/4/6/ 8/9	Home conflict, home dependency, wants reassurance only.
157–X	Lacks skills with the opposite sex, home conflict, mother conflict, sibling conflict, home dependency, wants reassurance only, nonresponsive or nonverbal, tense, indecisive, unhappy, worries a great deal, insomnia, confused. Note: Scale 5 coded high was infrequently associated with tension.
158–0	Home conflict, home dependency, lacks knowledge or information, aggressive or belligerent. This pattern was infrequently associated with introversion or self-consciousness or social insecurity, lack of skills with the opposite sex, being nonresponsive or nonverbal, tension.
158–2/3/4/6 7	Home conflict, home dependency.
158–9	Introverted or self-conscious or socially insecure, home conflict, home dependency.
158–X	Home conflict, home dependency, indecisive, unhappy, worries a great deal, insomnia, confused.
159–0	Mother conflict, home dependency, poor rapport. Note: Scale 0 coded

low was infrequently associated with poor rapport. This pattern was infrequently associated with introversion or self-consciousness or social insecurity, shyness in the interview, lack of skills with the opposite sex, being nonresponsive or nonverbal, being nonverbal or a nonrelator, tension, indecisiveness.

159–2/3	Mother conflict, home dependency, poor rapport.
159–4	Home conflict, mother conflict, home dependency, poor rapport.
159–6	Mother conflict, home dependency, poor rapport, rationalizes a great deal.
159–7/8	Mother conflict, home dependency, poor rapport.
159–X	Home conflict, mother conflict, home dependency, insomnia, poor rapport.
167–0	One interview only, lacks knowledge or information.
167–X	Lacks skills with the opposite sex, mother conflict, sibling conflict, nonresponsive or nonverbal, tense, indecisive, unhappy, worries a great deal, insomnia, confused.
168–0	Lacks knowledge or information, aggressive or belligerent.
168–9	Introverted or self-conscious or socially insecure.
168–X	Indecisive, unhappy, worries a great deal, insomnia, confused.
169–0	Aggressive or belligerent. This pattern was infrequently associated with introversion or self-consciousness or social insecurity, shyness in the interview, being nonresponsive or nonverbal, being nonverbal or a nonrelator, indecisiveness.
17–0	One interview only, lacks knowledge or information.
17–X	Lacks skills with the opposite sex, mother conflict, sibling conflict, nonresponsive or nonverbal, tense, indecisive, unhappy, worries a great deal, insomnia, confused.
178–0	Introverted or self-conscious or socially insecure, one interview only, nonresponsive or nonverbal, tense, indecisive, lacks knowledge or information, vague goals, confused, aggressive or belligerent. Note: Scale 0 coded low was infrequently associated with introversion or self-consciousness or social insecurity, being nonresponsive or nonverbal, indecisiveness.
178–2/3/4/5/ 6/9	Introverted or self-conscious or socially insecure, nonresponsive or nonverbal, tense, indecisive, lacks knowledge or information, vague goals, confused.
178–X	Introverted or self-conscious or socially insecure, lacks skills with the opposite sex, mother conflict, sibling conflict, nonresponsive or nonverbal, tense, indecisive, unhappy, worries a great deal, insomnia, lacks knowledge or information, vague goals, confused.
179–0	Home conflict, one interview only, lacks knowledge or information, aggressive or belligerent, defensive. This pattern was infrequently associated with introversion or self-consciousness or social insecurity, shyness in the interview, being nonresponsive or nonverbal, being nonverbal or a nonrelator, indecisiveness.
179–2/3/4/5	Home conflict, defensive.
179–6	Home conflict, defensive, rationalizes a great deal.
179–8	Home conflict, defensive.
179–X	Lacks skills with the opposite sex, home conflict, mother conflict, sibling

conflict, nonresponsive or nonverbal, tense, indecisive, unhappy, worries a great deal, insomnia, confused, defensive. Note: Scale 9 coded high was infrequently associated with indecisiveness, being nonresponsive or nonverbal, worrying a great deal, lack of skills with the opposite sex.

18–0   Lacks knowledge or information, aggressive or belligerent.

18–9   Introverted or self-conscious or socially insecure.

18–X   Indecisive, unhappy, worries a great deal, insomnia, confused.

189–0   Lacks knowledge or information, lacks academic motivation, aggressive or belligerent. This pattern was infrequently associated with introversion or self-consciousness or social insecurity, shyness in the interview, being nonresponsive or nonverbal, being nonverbal or a nonrelator, indecisiveness.

189–6   Rationalizes a great deal.

189–X   Indecisive, unhappy, worries a great deal, insomnia, confused. Note: Scale 9 coded high was infrequently associated with indecisiveness and worrying a great deal.

19–0   Aggressive or belligerent. This pattern was infrequently associated with introversion or self-consciousness or social insecurity, shyness in the interview, being nonresponsive or nonverbal, being nonverbal or a nonrelator, indecisiveness.

19–6   Rationalizes a great deal.

2–X   Introverted or self-conscious or socially insecure, lacks skills with the opposite sex, tense, unhappy, worries a great deal, insomnia.

23–0   One interview only, aggressive or belligerent, wants answers or insists on test scores. This pattern was infrequently associated with introversion or self-consciousness or social insecurity, lack of social skills, mother conflict, being nonresponsive or nonverbal, being nonverbal or a nonrelator, being unrealistic or illogical, nervousness, restlessness, unhappiness.

23–X   Introverted or self-conscious or socially insecure, lacks skills with the opposite sex, tense, unhappy, worries a great deal, insomnia.

234–0   Father conflict, one interview only, aggressive or belligerent, wants answers or insists on test scores. This pattern was infrequently associated with introversion or self-consciousness or social insecurity, lack of social skills, mother conflict, being nonresponsive or nonverbal, being nonverbal or a nonrelator, being unrealistic or illogical, nervousness, restlessness, unhappiness.

234–X   Introverted or self-conscious or socially insecure, lacks skills with the opposite sex, tense, unhappy, worries a great deal, insomnia. Note: Scale 4 coded high was infrequently associated with lack of skills with the opposite sex.

235–0   Home dependency, wants reassurance only, one interview only (3–0), four or more conferences (35), worries a great deal, aggressive or belligerent, wants answers or insists on test scores. Note: Scale 0 coded low was infrequently associated with worrying a great deal; Scale 5 coded high was infrequently associated with wanting answers or insisting on test scores. This pattern was infrequently associated with introversion or self-consciousness or social insecurity, lack of social skills, lack of skills with the opposite sex, mother conflict, being nonresponsive or nonverbal, being nonverbal or a nonrelator, being unrealistic or illogical, nervousness, restlessness, tension, unhappiness.

235–1   Home dependency, four or more conferences, wants reassurance only, restless, worries a great deal. Note: Scale 3 coded high was infrequently associated with restlessness.

235–4/6/7/8/9   Home dependency, four or more conferences, wants reassurance only, worries a great deal.

235–X   Introverted or self-conscious or socially insecure, lacks skills with the opposite sex, home conflict, home dependency, four or more conferences, wants reassurance only, tense, unhappy, worries a great deal, insomnia. Note: Scale 5 coded high was infrequently associated with tension.

236–0   One interview only, aggressive or belligerent, wants answers or insists on test scores. This pattern was infrequently associated with introversion or self-consciousness or social insecurity, lack of social skills, mother conflict, being nonreponsive or nonverbal, being nonverbal or a nonrelator, being unrealistic or illogical, nervousness, restlessness, unhappiness.

236–X   Introverted or self-conscious or socially insecure, lacks skills with the opposite sex, tense, unhappy, worries a great deal, insomnia.

237–0   One interview only, tense, tense on examinations, indecisive, unhappy (27), worries a great deal, lacks knowledge or information, aggressive or belligerent, wants answers or insists on test scores. Note: Scale 0 coded low was infrequently associated with indecisiveness, unhappiness, worrying a great deal. This pattern was infrequently associated with introversion or self-consciousness or social insecurity, lack of social skills, mother conflict, being nonresponsive or nonverbal, being nonverbal or a nonrelator, being unrealistic or illogical, nervousness, restlessness, unhappiness (3–0).

237–1   Home conflict, nonresponsive or nonverbal, tense, tense on examinations, indecisive, unhappy, worries a great deal, confused.

237–4/5/6/8   Tense, tense on examinations, indecisive, unhappy, worries a great deal.

237–9   Generally dependent, tense, tense on examinations, indecisive, unhappy, worries a great deal.

237–X   Introverted or self-conscious or socially insecure, lacks social skills, lacks skills with the opposite sex, home conflict, mother conflict, sibling conflict, nonresponsive or nonverbal, tense, tense on examinations, indecisive, unhappy, worries a great deal, insomnia, confused. Note: Scale 3 coded high was infrequently associated with mother conflict.

238–0   Introverted or self-conscious or socially insecure (28), lacks skills with the opposite sex, lacks knowledge or information, aggressive or belligerent, wants answers or insists on test scores, one interview only. Note: Scale 0 coded low was infrequently associated with lack of skills with the opposite sex. This pattern was infrequently associated with introversion or self-consciousness or social insecurity, lack of social skills, mother conflict, being nonresponsive or nonverbal, being nonverbal or a nonrelator, being unrealistic or illogical, nervousness, restlessness, unhappiness.

238–1/4/5/6/ 7   Introverted or self-conscious or socially insecure, lacks skills with the opposite sex, lacks knowledge or information.

238–9   Introverted or self-conscious or socially insecure, lacks skills with the opposite sex, lacks knowledge or information.

238–X   Introverted or self-conscious or socially insecure, lacks skills with the opposite sex, tense, indecisive, unhappy, worries a great deal, insomnia, lacks knowledge or information, confused.

239–0   One interview only, tense on examinations, aggressive or belligerent, wants answers or insists on test scores, rationalizes a great deal. This pattern was infrequently associated with introversion or self-consciousness or social insecurity, shyness in the interview, lack of social skills, mother conflict, being nonresponsive or nonverbal, being nonverbal or a nonrelator, being unrealistic or illogical, nervousness, restlessness, indecisiveness, unhappiness.

239–1/4/5/6/ 7/8   Tense on examinations, aggressive or belligerent, rationalizes a great deal.

239–X   Introverted or self-conscious or socially insecure, lacks skills with the opposite sex, tense on examinations, tense, unhappy, worries a great deal, insomnia, aggressive or belligerent, rationalizes a great deal. Note: Scale 9 coded high was infrequently associated with worrying a great deal and lack of skills with the opposite sex.

24–0   Father conflict, aggressive or belligerent.

24–X   Introverted or self-conscious or socially insecure, lacks skills with the opposite sex, tense, unhappy, worries a great deal, insomnia. Note: Scale 4 coded high was infrequently associated with lack of skills with the opposite sex.

245–0   Father conflict, wants reassurance only, worries a great deal, aggressive or belligerent. Note: Scale 0 coded low was infrequently associated with worrying a great deal. This pattern was infrequently associated with introversion or self-consciousness or social insecurity, lack of skills with the opposite sex, being nonresponsive or nonverbal, tension.

245–1   Home conflict, wants reassurance only, restless, worries a great deal.

245–3/6/7/8/ 9   Wants reassurance only, worries a great deal.

245–X   Introverted or self-conscious or socially insecure, lacks skills with the opposite sex, home conflict, wants reassurance only, tense, unhappy, worries a great deal, insomnia. Note: Scale 5 coded high was infrequently associated with tension; Scale 4 coded high was infrequently associated with lack of skills with the opposite sex.

246–0   Father conflict, worries a great deal, aggressive or belligerent. Note: Scale 0 coded low was infrequently associated with worrying a great deal.

246–1/3/5/7/ 8/9   Worries a great deal.

246–X   Introverted or self-conscious or socially insecure, lacks skills with the opposite sex, tense, unhappy, worries a great deal, insomnia. Note: Scale 4 coded high was infrequently associated with lack of skills with the opposite sex.

247–0   Home conflict, father conflict, one interview only, tense, tense on examinations, indecisive, unhappy, worries a great deal, lacks knowledge or information, aggressive or belligerent. Note: Scale 0 coded low was infrequently associated with indecisiveness, unhappiness, and worrying a great deal.

247–1 Home conflict, nonresponsive or nonverbal, tense, tense on examinations, indecisive, unhappy, worries a great deal, confused.

247–3/5/6/8 Home conflict, tense, tense on examinations, indecisive, unhappy, worries a great deal.

247–9 Home conflict, generally dependent, tense, tense on examinations, indecisive, unhappy, worries a great deal.

247–X Introverted or self-conscious or socially insecure, lacks social skills, lacks skills with the opposite sex, home conflict, mother conflict, sibling conflict, nonresponsive or nonverbal, tense, tense on examinations, indecisive, unhappy, worries a great deal, insomnia, confused, poor rapport. Note: Scale 4 coded high was infrequently associated with lack of skills with the opposite sex.

248–0 Introverted or self-conscious or socially insecure (28), lacks skills with the opposite sex, father conflict, lacks knowledge or information, aggressive or belligerent. Note: Both Scale 4 coded high and Scale 0 coded low were infrequently associated with lack of skills with the opposite sex; Scale 0 coded low was infrequently associated with introversion or self-consciousness or social insecurity.

248–1/3/5/6/ Introverted or self-conscious or socially insecure, lacks skills with the
7 opposite sex. Note: Scale 4 coded high was infrequently associated with lack of skills with the opposite sex.

248–9 Introverted or self-conscious or socially insecure, lacks skills with the opposite sex. Note: Scale 4 coded high was infrequently associated with lack of skills with the opposite sex.

248–X Introverted or self-conscious or socially insecure, lacks skills with the opposite sex, tense, indecisive, unhappy, worries a great deal, insomnia, confused. Note: Scale 4 coded high was infrequently associated with lack of skills with the opposite sex.

249–0 Father conflict, tense on examinations, aggressive or belligerent, rationalizes a great deal. This pattern was infrequently associated with introversion or self-consciousness or social insecurity, shyness in the interview, being nonresponsive or nonverbal, being nonverbal or a nonrelator, indecisiveness.

249–1/3/5/6/ Tense on examinations, aggressive or belligerent, rationalizes a great
7/8 deal.

249–X Introverted or self-conscious or socially insecure, lacks skills with the opposite sex, tense, tense on examinations, unhappy, worries a great deal, insomnia, aggressive or belligerent, rationalizes a great deal. Note: Scales 4 and 9 coded high were infrequently associated with lack of skills with the opposite sex; Scale 9 was infrequently associated with worrying a great deal.

25–0 Wants reassurance only, worries a great deal. Note: Scale 0 coded low was infrequently associated with worrying a great deal. This pattern was infrequently associated with introversion or self-consciousness or social insecurity, lack of skills with the opposite sex, being nonresponsive or nonverbal, tension.

25–1 Wants reassurance only, worries a great deal, restless.

25–3/4/6/7/ Wants reassurance only, worries a great deal.
8/9

25–X Introverted or self-conscious or socially insecure, lacks skills with the opposite sex, home conflict, wants reassurance only, tense, unhappy, worries a great deal, insomnia. Note: Scale 5 coded high was infrequently associated with tension.

256–0 Wants reassurance only, worries a great deal. Note: Scale 0 coded low was infrequently associated with worrying a great deal. This pattern was infrequently associated with introversion or self-consciousness or social insecurity, lack of skills with the opposite sex, being nonresponsive or nonverbal, tension.

256–1 Wants reassurance only, worries a great deal, restless.

256–3/4/7/8/ Wants reassurance only, worries a great deal.
9

256–X Introverted or self-conscious or socially insecure, lacks skills with the opposite sex, home conflict, wants reassurance only, tense, unhappy, worries a great deal, insomnia. Note: Scale 5 coded high was infrequently associated with tension.

257–0 Home conflict, one interview only, wants reassurance only, tense (27), tense on examinations, indecisive, unhappy, worries a great deal, lacks knowledge or information. Note: Scale 0 coded low was infrequently associated with indecisiveness, unhappiness, and worrying a great deal. This pattern was infrequently associated with introversion or self-consciousness or social insecurity, lack of skills with the opposite sex, being nonresponsive or nonverbal, tension (5–0).

257–1 Home conflict, wants reassurance only, nonresponsive or nonverbal, restless, tense, tense on examinations, indecisive, unhappy, worries a great deal, confused. Note: Scale 5 coded high was infrequently associated with tension.

257–3/4/6/8/ Home conflict, wants reassurance only, tense, tense on examinations,
9 indecisive, unhappy, worries a great deal. Note: Scale 5 coded high was infrequently associated with tension.

257–X Introverted or self-conscious or socially insecure, lacks social skills, lacks skills with the opposite sex, home conflict, mother conflict, sibling conflict, wants reassurance only, nonresponsive or nonverbal, tense, tense on examinations, indecisive, unhappy, worries a great deal, insomnia, confused. Note: Scale 5 coded high was infrequently associated with tension.

258–0 Introverted or self-conscious or socially insecure (28), lacks skills with the opposite sex (28), home conflict, wants reassurance only, worries a great deal, lacks knowledge or information, aggressive or belligerent. Note: Scale 0 coded low was infrequently associated with lack of skills with the opposite sex and worrying a great deal. This pattern was infrequently associated with introversion or self-consciousness or social insecurity (5–0), lack of skills with the opposite sex (5–0), being nonresponsive or nonverbal, tension.

258–1	Introverted or self-conscious or socially insecure, lacks skills with the opposite sex, home conflict, wants reassurance only, restless, worries a great deal.
258–3/4/6/7	Introverted or self-conscious or socially insecure, lacks skills with the opposite sex, home conflict, worries a great deal, wants reassurance only.
258–9	Introverted or self-conscious or socially insecure, lacks skills with the opposite sex, home conflict, worries a great deal, wants reassurance only.
258–X	Introverted or self-conscious or socially insecure, lacks skills with the opposite sex, home conflict, wants reassurance only, tense, indecisive, unhappy, worries a great deal, insomnia, confused. Note: Scale 5 coded high was infrequently associated with tension.
259–0	Mother conflict, wants reassurance only, tense on examinations, worries a great deal, poor rapport, aggressive or belligerent, rationalizes a great deal. Note: Scale 0 coded low was infrequently associated with poor rapport and worrying a great deal. This pattern was infrequently associated with introversion or self-consciousness or social insecurity, shyness in the interview, lack of skills with the opposite sex, being nonresponsive or nonverbal, being nonverbal or a nonrelator, tension, indecisiveness.
259–1	Mother conflict, wants reassurance only, restless, tense on examinations, worries a great deal, poor rapport, aggressive or belligerent, rationalizes a great deal. Note: Scale 9 coded high was infrequently associated with worrying a great deal.
259–3/4/6/7/ 8	Mother conflict, wants reassurance only, tense on examinations, worries a great deal, poor rapport, aggressive or belligerent, rationalizes a great deal. Note: Scale 9 coded high was infrequently associated with worrying a great deal.
259–X	Introverted or self-conscious or socially insecure, lacks skills with the opposite sex, home conflict, mother conflict, wants reassurance only, tense, tense on examinations, unhappy, worries a great deal, insomnia, poor rapport, aggressive or belligerent, rationalizes a great deal. Note: Scale 9 coded high was infrequently associated with lack of skills with the opposite sex and worrying a great deal; Scale 5 coded high was infrequently associated with tension.
26–X	Introverted or self-conscious or socially insecure, lacks skills with the opposite sex, tense, unhappy, worries a great deal, insomnia.
267–0	Tense, tense on examinations, indecisive, unhappy, worries a great deal, lacks knowledge or information, one interview only. Note: Scale 0 coded low was infrequently associated with indecisiveness, unhappiness, worrying a great deal.
267–1	Tense, tense on examinations, indecisive, unhappy, worries a great deal, confused, nonresponsive or nonverbal, home conflict.
267–3/4/5/8	Tense, tense on examinations, indecisive, unhappy, worries a great deal.
267–9	Tense, tense on examinations, indecisive, unhappy, worries a great deal, generally dependent.
267–X	Introverted or self-conscious or socially insecure, lacks social skills, lacks skills with the opposite sex, home conflict, mother conflict, sibling conflict, tense, tense on examinations, indecisive, unhappy, worries a great deal, insomnia, confused, nonresponsive or nonverbal.

268–0	Introverted or self-conscious or socially insecure (28), lacks skills with the opposite sex, lacks knowledge or information, aggressive or belligerent. Note: Scale 0 coded low was infrequently associated with introversion or self-consciousness or social insecurity, lack of skills with the opposite sex.
268–1/3/4/5/ 7	Lacks skills with the opposite sex, introverted or self-conscious or socially insecure.
268–9	Introverted or self-conscious or socially insecure, lacks skills with the opposite sex.
268–X	Introverted or self-conscious or socially insecure, lacks skills with the opposite sex, tense, indecisive, unhappy, worries a great deal, insomnia, confused.
269–0	Tense on examinations, aggressive or belligerent, rationalizes a great deal. This pattern was infrequently associated with introversion or self-consciousness or social insecurity, shyness in the interview, being nonresponsive or nonverbal, being nonverbal or a nonrelator, indecisiveness.
269–1/3/4/5/ 7/8	Tense on examinations, aggressive or belligerent, rationalizes a great deal.
269–X	Introverted or self-conscious or socially insecure, lacks skills with the opposite sex, tense, tense on examinations, unhappy, worries a great deal, insomnia, aggressive or belligerent, rationalizes a great deal. Note: Scale 9 coded high was infrequently associated with worrying a great deal and lack of skills with the opposite sex.
27–0	One interview only, tense, tense on examinations, indecisive, unhappy, worries a great deal, lacks knowledge or information. Note: Scale 0 coded low was infrequently associated with indecisiveness, unhappiness, worrying a great deal.
27–1	Tense, tense on examinations, indecisive, unhappy, worries a great deal, confused, nonresponsive or nonverbal, home conflict.
27–3/4/5/6/ 8	Tense, tense on examinations, indecisive, unhappy, worries a great deal.
27–9	Tense, tense on examinations, indecisive, unhappy, worries a great deal, generally dependent.
27–X	Introverted or self-conscious or socially insecure, lacks social skills, lacks skills with the opposite sex, home conflict, mother conflict, sibling conflict, nonresponsive or nonverbal, tense, tense on examinations, indecisive, unhappy, worries a great deal, insomnia, confused.
278–0	Introverted or self-conscious or socially insecure, lacks skills with the opposite sex, one interview only, nonresponsive or nonverbal, tense, tense on examinations, indecisive, unhappy, worries a great deal, lacks knowledge or information, vague goals, confused, aggressive or belligerent. Note: Scale 0 coded low was infrequently associated with introversion or self-consciousness or social insecurity, lack of skills with the opposite sex, being nonresponsive or nonverbal, indecisiveness, unhappiness, worrying a great deal.
278–1/3/4/5/ 6	Introverted or self-conscious or socially insecure, lacks skills with the opposite sex, nonresponsive or nonverbal, tense, tense on examinations, indecisive, unhappy, worries a great deal, lacks knowledge or information, vague goals, confused.

MALE SECTION

278–9 Introverted or self-conscious or socially insecure, lacks skills with the opposite sex, generally dependent, nonresponsive or nonverbal, tense, tense on examinations, indecisive, unhappy, worries a great deal, lacks knowledge or information, vague goals, confused.

278–X Introverted or self-conscious or socially insecure, lacks social skills, lacks skills with the opposite sex, home conflict, mother conflict, sibling conflict, nonresponsive or nonverbal, tense, tense on examinations, indecisive, unhappy, worries a great deal, insomnia, lacks knowledge or information, vague goals, confused.

279–0 Home conflict, one interview only, tense, tense on examinations, indecisive (27), unhappy, worries a great deal, lacks knowledge or information, aggressive or belligerent, rationalizes a great deal, defensive. Note: Scale 0 coded low was infrequently associated with indecisiveness, unhappiness, worrying a great deal; Scale 9 coded high was infrequently associated with worrying a great deal. This pattern was infrequently associated with introversion or self-consciousness or social insecurity, shyness in the interview, being nonresponsive or nonverbal, being nonverbal or a nonrelator, indecisiveness (9–0).

279–1 Home conflict, nonresponsive or nonverbal, tense, tense on examinations, indecisive, unhappy, worries a great deal, confused, aggressive or belligerent, rationalizes a great deal, defensive. Note: Scale 9 coded high was infrequently associated with being nonresponsive or nonverbal, indecisiveness, worrying a great deal.

279–3/4/5/6/ 8 Home conflict, tense, tense on examinations, indecisive, unhappy, worries a great deal, aggressive or belligerent, rationalizes a great deal, defensive. Note: Scale 9 coded high was infrequently associated with indecisiveness and worrying a great deal.

279–X Introverted or self-conscious or socially insecure, lacks social skills, lacks skills with the opposite sex, home conflict, mother conflict, sibling conflict, nonresponsive or nonverbal, tense, tense on examinations, indecisive, unhappy, worries a great deal, insomnia, confused, aggressive or belligerent, rationalizes a great deal, defensive. Note: Scale 9 coded high was infrequently associated with lack of skills with the opposite sex, being nonresponsive or nonverbal, indecisiveness, worrying a great deal.

28–0 Introverted or self-conscious or socially insecure (28), lacks skills with the opposite sex, lacks knowledge or information, aggressive or belligerent. Note: Scale 0 coded low was infrequently associated with introversion or self-consciousness or social insecurity, lack of skills with the opposite sex.

28–1 Introverted or self-conscious or socially insecure, lacks skills with the opposite sex.

28–3/4/5/6/ 7 Lacks skills with the opposite sex.

28–9 Introverted or self-conscious or socially insecure, lacks skills with the opposite sex.

28–X Introverted or self-conscious or socially insecure, lacks skills with the opposite sex, indecisive, tense, unhappy, worries a great deal, insomnia, confused.

289–0 Introverted or self-conscious or socially insecure (28), lacks skills with

57

the opposite sex, tense on examinations, lacks knowledge or information, lacks academic motivation, aggressive or belligerent, rationalizes a great deal. Note: Both Scale 9 coded high and Scale 0 coded low were infrequently associated with lack of skills with the opposite sex. This pattern was infrequently associated with introversion or self-consciousness or social insecurity (9–0), shyness in the interview, being nonresponsive or nonverbal, being nonverbal or a nonrelator, indecisiveness.

289–1/3/4/5/ 6/7 — Introverted or self-conscious or socially insecure, lacks skills with the opposite sex, tense on examinations, aggressive or belligerent, rationalizes a great deal. Note: Scale 9 coded high was infrequently associated with lack of skills with the opposite sex.

289–X — Introverted or self-conscious or socially insecure, lacks skills with the opposite sex, tense, tense on examinations, indecisive, unhappy, worries a great deal, insomnia, confused, aggressive or belligerent, rationalizes a great deal. Note: Scale 9 coded high was infrequently associated with lack of skills with the opposite sex, indecisiveness, worrying a great deal.

29–0 — Tense on examinations, aggressive or belligerent, rationalizes a great deal. This pattern was infrequently associated with introversion or self-consciousness or social insecurity, shyness in the interview, being nonresponsive or nonverbal, being nonverbal or a nonrelator, indecisiveness.

29–1/3/4/5/ 6/7/8 — Tense on examinations, aggressive or belligerent, rationalizes a great deal.

29–X — Introverted or self-conscious or socially insecure, lacks skills with the opposite sex, tense, tense on examinations, unhappy, worries a great deal, insomnia, aggressive or belligerent, rationalizes a great deal. Note: Scale 9 coded high was infrequently associated with worrying a great deal and lack of skills with the opposite sex.

3–0 — One interview only, aggressive or belligerent, wants answers or insists on test scores. This pattern was infrequently associated with introversion or self-consciousness or social insecurity, lack of social skills, mother conflict, being nonresponsive or nonverbal, being nonverbal or a nonrelator, being unrealistic or illogical, nervousness, restlessness, unhappiness.

34–0 — Father conflict, one interview only, aggressive or belligerent, wants answers or insists on test scores. This pattern was infrequently associated with introversion or self-consciousness or social insecurity, lack of social skills, mother conflict, being nonresponsive or nonverbal, being nonverbal or a nonrelator, being unrealistic or illogical, nervousness, restlessness, unhappiness.

345–0 — Father conflict, home dependency, one interview only (3–0), four or more conferences (35), aggressive or belligerent, wants answers or insists on test scores. Note: Scale 5 coded high was infrequently associated with wanting answers or insisting on test scores. This pattern was infrequently associated with introversion or self-consciousness or social insecurity, lack of social skills, lack of skills with the opposite sex, mother conflict, being nonresponsive or nonverbal, being nonverbal or a nonrelator, being unrealistic or illogical, nervousness, tension, restlessness, unhappiness.

MALE SECTION

345–1   Home conflict, home dependency, four or more conferences, restless. Note: Scale 3 coded high was infrequently associated with restlessness.

345–2/6/7/8/ Home dependency, four or more conferences.
    9

345–X   Lacks skills with the opposite sex, home conflict, home dependency, four or more conferences, insomnia. Note: Scale 4 coded high was infrequently associated with lack of skills with the opposite sex.

346–0   Father conflict, one interview only, worries a great deal, aggressive or belligerent, wants answers or insists on test scores. Note: Scale 0 coded low was infrequently associated with worrying a great deal. This pattern was infrequently associated with introversion or self-consciousness or social insecurity, lack of social skills, mother conflict, being nonresponsive or nonverbal, being nonverbal or a nonrelator, being unrealistic or illogical, nervousness, restlessness, unhappiness.

346–1/2/5/7/ Worries a great deal.
  8/9/X

347–0   Home conflict, father conflict, one interview only, lacks knowledge or information, aggressive or belligerent, wants answers or insists on test scores. This pattern was infrequently associated with lack of social skills, mother conflict, being nonresponsive or nonverbal, being nonverbal or a nonrelator, being unrealistic or illogical, nervousness, restlessness, unhappiness.

347–1/2/5/6/ Home conflict.
  8/9

347–X   Lacks skills with the opposite sex, home conflict, mother conflict, sibling conflict, nonresponsive or nonverbal, tense, indecisive, unhappy, worries a great deal, insomnia, confused, poor rapport. Note: Scale 3 coded high was infrequently associated with mother conflict; Scale 4 coded high was infrequently associated with lack of skills with the opposite sex.

348–0   Father conflict, one interview only, lacks knowledge or information, aggressive or belligerent, wants answers or insists on test scores. This pattern was infrequently associated with introversion or self-consciousness or social insecurity, lack of social skills, mother conflict, being nonresponsive or nonverbal, being nonverbal or a nonrelator, being unrealistic or illogical, nervousness, restlessness, unhappiness.

348–1/2/5/6/ Lacks knowledge or information.
  7

348–9   Introverted or self-conscious or socially insecure, lacks knowledge or information.

348–X   Indecisive, unhappy, worries a great deal, insomnia, lacks knowledge or information, confused.

349–0   Father conflict, one interview only, aggressive or belligerent, wants answers or insists on test scores. This pattern was infrequently associated with introversion or self-consciousness or social insecurity, shyness in the interview, lack of social skills, mother conflict, being nonresponsive or nonverbal, being nonverbal or a nonrelator, being unrealistic or illogical, nervousness, restlessness, indecisiveness, unhappiness.

349–2   Aggressive or belligerent.

349–6   Rationalizes a great deal.

CODEBOOK OF MMPI PATTERNS

35–0   Home dependency, one interview only (3–0), four or more conferences (35), aggressive or belligerent, wants answers or insists on test scores. Note: Scale 5 coded high was infrequently associated with wanting answers or insisting on test scores. This pattern was infrequently associated with introversion or self-consciousness or social insecurity, lack of social skills, lack of skills with the opposite sex, mother conflict, being nonresponsive or nonverbal, being nonverbal or a nonrelator, being unrealistic or illogical, nervousness, restlessness, tension, unhappiness.

35–1   Home dependency, four or more conferences, restless. Note: Scale 3 coded high was infrequently associated with restlessness.

35–2/4/6/7/ Home dependency, four or more conferences.
8/9

35–X   Home dependency, home conflict, four or more conferences, lacks skills with the opposite sex, insomnia.

356–0   Home dependency, one interview only (3–0), four or more conferences (35), aggressive or belligerent, wants answers or insists on test scores. Note: Scale 5 coded high was infrequently associated with wanting answers or insisting on test scores. This pattern was infrequently associated with introversion or self-consciousness or social insecurity, lack of social skills, lack of skills with the opposite sex, mother conflict, being nonresponsive or nonverbal, being nonverbal or a nonrelator, being unrealistic or illogical, nervousness, restlessness, tension, unhappiness.

356–1   Home dependency, four or more conferences, restless. Note: Scale 3 coded high was infrequently associated with restlessness.

356–2/4/7/8/ Home dependency, four or more conferences.
9

356–X   Home dependency, home conflict, four or more conferences, lacks skills with the opposite sex, insomnia.

357–0   Home conflict, home dependency, one interview only (3–0), four or more conferences (35), wants reassurance only, lacks knowledge or information, aggressive or belligerent, wants answers or insists on test scores. Note: Scale 5 coded high was infrequently associated with wanting answers or insisting on test scores. This pattern was infrequently associated with introversion or self-consciousness or social insecurity, lack of social skills, lack of skills with the opposite sex, mother conflict, being nonresponsive or nonverbal, being nonverbal or a nonrelator, being unrealistic or illogical, nervousness, restlessness, tension, unhappiness.

357–1   Home conflict, home dependency, four or more conferences, wants reassurance only, nonresponsive or nonverbal, restless. Note: Scale 3 coded high was infrequently associated with restlessness.

357–2/4/6/8/ Home conflict, home dependency, four or more conferences, wants
9   reassurance only.

357–X   Home conflict, home dependency, mother conflict, sibling conflict, four or more conferences, wants reassurance only, lacks skills with the opposite sex, nonresponsive or nonverbal, tense, indecisive, unhappy, worries a great deal, insomnia, confused. Note: Scale 3 coded high was infrequently associated with mother conflict; Scale 5 coded high was infrequently associated with tension.

358–0   Home conflict, home dependency, one interview only (3–0), four or more conferences (35), aggressive or belligerent, wants answers or insists on test scores. Note: Scale 5 coded high was infrequently associated with wanting answers or insisting on test scores. This pattern was infrequently associated with introversion or self-consciousness or social insecurity, lack of social skills, lack of skills with the opposite sex, mother conflict, being nonresponsive or nonverbal, being nonverbal or a nonrelator, being unrealistic or illogical, nervousness, restlessness, tension, unhappiness.

358–1   Home conflict, home dependency, four or more conferences, lacks knowledge or information, restless. Note: Scale 3 coded high was infrequently associated with restlessness.

358–2/4/6/7   Home conflict, home dependency, four or more conferences, lacks knowledge or information.

358–9   Home conflict, home dependency, four or more conferences, lacks knowledge or information, introverted or self-conscious or socially insecure.

358–X   Home conflict, home dependency, four or more conferences, lacks knowledge or information, confused, unhappy, worries a great deal, insomnia, lacks skills with the opposite sex, indecisive.

359–0   Home dependency, one interview only (3–0), four or more conferences (35), poor rapport, aggressive or belligerent, wants answers or insists on test scores, mother conflict (59). Note: Scale 0 coded low was infrequently associated with poor rapport; Scale 5 coded high was infrequently associated with wanting answers or insisting on test scores. This pattern was infrequently associated with introversion or self-consciousness or social insecurity, shyness in the interview, lack of social skills, lack of skills with the opposite sex, mother conflict (3–0), being nonresponsive or nonverbal, being nonverbal or a nonrelator, being unrealistic or illogical, nervousness, restlessness, tension, indecisiveness, unhappiness.

359–1   Home dependency, mother conflict, four or more conferences, poor rapport, restless. Note: Scale 3 coded high was infrequently associated with mother conflict and restlessness.

359–2/4   Home dependency, mother conflict, four or more conferences, poor rapport. Note: Scale 3 coded high was infrequently associated with mother conflict.

359–6   Home dependency, mother conflict, four or more conferences, poor rapport, rationalizes a great deal. Note: Scale 3 coded high was infrequently associated with mother conflict.

359–7/8   Home dependency, mother conflict, four or more conferences, poor rapport. Note: Scale 3 coded high was infrequently associated with mother conflict.

359–X   Lacks skills with the opposite sex, home conflict, mother conflict, home dependency, four or more conferences, insomnia, poor rapport. Note: Scale 3 coded high was infrequently associated with mother conflict.

36–0   One interview only, aggressive or belligerent, wants answers or insists on test scores. This pattern was infrequently associated with introversion or self-consciousness or social insecurity, lack of social skills, mother conflict, being nonresponsive or nonverbal, being nonverbal or a non-relator, being unrealistic or illogical, nervousness, restlessness, unhappiness.

367–0 One interview only, aggressive or belligerent, wants answers or insists on test scores, lacks knowledge or information. This pattern was infrequently associated with introversion or self-consciousness or social insecurity, lack of social skills, mother conflict, being nonresponsive or nonverbal, being nonverbal or a nonrelator, being unrealistic or illogical, nervousness, restlessness, unhappiness.

367–1 Nonresponsive or nonverbal, home conflict.

367–X Lacks skills with the opposite sex, mother conflict, sibling conflict, nonresponsive or nonverbal, tense, indecisive, unhappy, worries a great deal, insomnia, confused. Note: Scale 3 coded high was infrequently associated with mother conflict.

368–0 One interview only, lacks knowledge or information, aggressive or belligerent, wants answers or insists on test scores. This pattern was infrequently associated with introversion or self-consciousness or social insecurity, lack of social skills, mother conflict, being nonresponsive or nonverbal, being nonverbal or a nonrelator, being unrealistic or illogical, nervousness, restlessness, unhappiness.

368–1/2/4/5/ 7 Lacks knowledge or information.

368–9 Introverted or self-conscious or socially insecure, lacks knowledge or information.

368–X Indecisive, unhappy, worries a great deal, insomnia, lacks knowledge or information, confused.

369–0 One interview only, aggressive or belligerent, wants answers or insists on test scores. This pattern was infrequently associated with introversion or self-consciousness or social insecurity, shyness in the interview, lack of social skills, mother conflict, being nonresponsive or nonverbal, being nonverbal or a nonrelator, being unrealistic or illogical, nervousness, restlessness, indecisiveness, unhappiness.

37–0 One interview only, lacks knowledge or information, aggressive or belligerent, wants answers or insists on test scores. This pattern was infrequently associated with introversion or self-consciousness or social insecurity, lack of social skills, mother conflict, being nonresponsive or nonverbal, being nonverbal or a nonrelator, being unrealistic or illogical, nervousness, restlessness, unhappiness.

37–X Lacks skills with the opposite sex, mother conflict, sibling conflict, nonresponsive or nonverbal, tense, indecisive, unhappy, worries a great deal, insomnia, confused. Note: Scale 3 coded high was infrequently associated with mother conflict.

378–0 Introverted or self-conscious or socially insecure (78), one interview only, nonresponsive or nonverbal (78), tense, indecisive, lacks knowledge or information, vague goals, confused, aggressive or belligerent, wants answers or insists on test scores. Note: Scale 0 coded low was infrequently associated with indecisiveness. This pattern was infrequently associated with introversion or self-consciousness or social insecurity (3–0), lack of social skills, mother conflict, being nonresponsive or nonverbal (3–0), being nonverbal or a nonrelator, being unrealistic or illogical, nervousness, restlessness, unhappiness.

378–1/2/4/5/ 6/9   Introverted or self-conscious or socially insecure, nonresponsive or non-verbal, tense, indecisive, lacks knowledge or information, vague goals, confused.

378–X   Introverted or self-conscious or socially insecure, lacks skills with the opposite sex, mother conflict, sibling conflict, nonresponsive or non-verbal, tense, indecisive, unhappy, worries a great deal, insomnia, lacks knowledge or information, vague goals, confused. Note: Scale 3 coded high was infrequently associated with mother conflict.

379–0   Home conflict, one interview only, lacks knowledge or information, aggressive or belligerent, wants answers or insists on test scores, defensive. This pattern was infrequently associated with introversion or self-consciousness or social insecurity, shyness in the interview, lack of social skills, mother conflict, being nonresponsive or nonverbal, being nonverbal or a nonrelator, being unrealistic or illogical, nervousness, restlessness, indecisiveness, unhappiness.

379–1   Home conflict, defensive, nonresponsive or nonverbal. Note: Scale 9 coded high was infrequently associated with being nonresponsive or nonverbal.

379–2/4/5/6/ 8   Home conflict, defensive.

379–X   Lacks skills with the opposite sex, home conflict, mother conflict, sibling conflict, nonresponsive or nonverbal, tense, indecisive, unhappy, worries a great deal, insomnia, confused, defensive. Note: Scale 3 coded high was infrequently associated with mother conflict; Scale 9 coded high was infrequently associated with lack of skills with the opposite sex, being nonresponsive or nonverbal, indecisiveness, worrying a great deal.

38–0   One interview only, lacks knowledge or information, aggressive or belligerent, wants answers or insists on test scores. This pattern was infrequently associated with introversion or self-consciousness or social insecurity, lack of social skills, mother conflict, being nonresponsive or nonverbal, being nonverbal or a nonrelator, being unrealistic or illogical, nervousness, restlessness, unhappiness.

38–1/2/4/5/ 6/7   Lacks knowledge or information.

38–9   Lacks knowledge or information, introverted or self-conscious or socially insecure.

38–X   Lacks knowledge or information, confused, unhappy, worries a great deal, insomnia, indecisive.

389–0   One interview only, aggressive or belligerent, wants answers or insists on test scores, lacks knowledge or information, lacks academic motivation. This pattern was infrequently associated with introversion or self-consciousness or social insecurity, shyness in the interview, lack of social skills, mother conflict, being nonresponsive or nonverbal, being nonverbal or a nonrelator, being unrealistic or illogical, nervousness, restlessness, indecisiveness, unhappiness.

389–1/2/4/5   Lacks knowledge or information.

389–6   Lacks knowledge or information, rationalizes a great deal.

CODEBOOK OF MMPI PATTERNS

389–7	Lacks knowledge or information.
389–X	Indecisive, unhappy, worries a great deal, confused, insomnia, lacks knowledge or information. Note: Scale 9 coded high was infrequently associated with indecisiveness and worrying a great deal.
39–0	One interview only, aggressive or belligerent, wants answers or insists on test scores. This pattern was infrequently associated with introversion or self-consciousness or social insecurity, shyness in the interview, lack of social skills, mother conflict, being nonresponsive or nonverbal, being nonverbal or a nonrelator, being unrealistic or illogical, nervousness, restlessness, indecisiveness, unhappiness.
39–6	Rationalizes a great deal.
4–0	Father conflict, aggressive or belligerent.
45–0	Father conflict, aggressive or belligerent. This pattern was infrequently associated with introversion or self-consciousness or social insecurity, lack of skills with the opposite sex, being nonresponsive or a nonrelator, tension.
45–1	Home conflict, restless.
45–X	Home conflict, insomnia.
456–0	Father conflict, aggressive or belligerent, worries a great deal. Note: Scale 0 coded low was infrequently associated with worrying a great deal. This pattern was infrequently associated with introversion or self-consciousness or social insecurity, lack of skills with the opposite sex, being nonresponsive or a nonrelator, tension.
456–1	Home conflict, worries a great deal, restless.
456–2/3/7/8/ 9	Worries a great deal.
456–X	Home conflict, worries a great deal, insomnia.
457–0	Home conflict, father conflict, one interview only, wants reassurance only, aggressive or belligerent, lacks knowledge or information.
457–1	Home conflict, wants reassurance only, nonresponsive or nonverbal, restless.
457–2/3/6/8/ 9	Home conflict, wants reassurance only.
457–X	Lacks skills with the opposite sex, home conflict, mother conflict, sibling conflict, wants reassurance only, nonresponsive or nonverbal, tense, indecisive, unhappy, worries a great deal, insomnia, confused, poor rapport. Note: Scale 5 coded high was infrequently associated with tension; Scale 4 coded high was infrequently associated with lack of skills with the opposite sex.
458–0	Home conflict, father conflict, aggressive or belligerent, lacks knowledge or information. This pattern was infrequently associated with introversion or self-consciousness or social insecurity, lack of skills with the opposite sex, being nonresponsive or nonverbal, tension.
458–1	Home conflict, restless.
458–2/3/6/7	Home conflict.
458–9	Home conflict, introverted or self-conscious or socially insecure.
458–X	Home conflict, indecisive, unhappy, worries a great deal, insomnia, confused.
459–0	Father conflict, mother conflict, poor rapport, aggressive or belligerent.

MALE SECTION

Note: Scale 0 coded low was infrequently associated with poor rapport. This pattern was infrequently associated with introversion or self-consciousness or social insecurity, shyness in the interview, lack of skills with the opposite sex, being nonresponsive or nonverbal, being nonverbal or a nonrelator, indecisiveness, tension.

459–1	Home conflict, mother conflict, restless, poor rapport.
459–2/3	Mother conflict, poor rapport.
459–6	Mother conflict, poor rapport, rationalizes a great deal.
459–7/8	Mother conflict, poor rapport.
459–X	Mother conflict, home conflict, poor rapport, insomnia.
46–0	Father conflict, worries a great deal, aggressive or belligerent. Note: Scale 0 coded low was infrequently associated with worrying a great deal.
46–1/2/3/5/ 7/8/9/X	Worries a great deal.
467–0	Introverted or self-conscious or socially insecure, home conflict, father conflict, one interview only, worries a great deal, lacks knowledge or information, aggressive or belligerent. Note: Scale 0 coded low was infrequently associated with worrying a great deal.
467–1	Introverted or self-conscious or socially insecure, home conflict, nonresponsive or nonverbal, worries a great deal.
467–2/3/5/8/ 9	Introverted or self-conscious or socially insecure, home conflict, worries a great deal.
467–X	Introverted or self-conscious or socially insecure, lacks skills with the opposite sex, home conflict, mother conflict, sibling conflict, nonresponsive or nonverbal, tense, indecisive, unhappy, worries a great deal, insomnia, confused, poor rapport. Note: Scale 4 coded high was infrequently associated with lack of skills with the opposite sex.
468–0	Father conflict, worries a great deal, lacks knowledge or information, aggressive or belligerent. Note: Scale 0 coded low was infrequently associated with worrying a great deal.
468–1/2/3/5	Worries a great deal.
468–9	Worries a great deal, introverted or self-conscious or socially insecure.
468–X	Worries a great deal, unhappy, insomnia, confused, indecisive.
469–0	Father conflict, worries a great deal, aggressive or belligerent. Note: Scale 0 coded low was infrequently associated with worrying a great deal. This pattern was infrequently associated with introversion of self-consciousness or social insecurity, shyness in the interview, being nonresponsive or nonverbal, being nonverbal or a nonrelator, indecisiveness.
469–1/2/3/5/ 7/8/X	Worries a great deal.
47–0	Home conflict, father conflict, one interview only, lacks knowledge or information, aggressive or belligerent.
47–1	Home conflict, nonresponsive or nonverbal.
47–2/3/5/6/ 8/9	Home conflict.
47–X	Lacks skills with the opposite sex, home conflict, mother conflict, sibling conflict, nonresponsive or nonverbal, tense, indecisive, unhappy, worries a great deal, insomnia, confused, poor rapport. Note: Scale 4 coded high was infrequently associated with lack of skills with the opposite sex.

CODEBOOK OF MMPI PATTERNS

478–0   Home conflict, father conflict, one interview only, nonresponsive or nonverbal, tense, indecisive, lacks knowledge or information, vague goals, confused, aggressive or belligerent. Note: Scale 0 coded low was infrequently associated with being nonresponsive or nonverbal, indecisiveness.

478–1/2/3/5/   Home conflict, nonresponsive or nonverbal, tense, indecisive, lacks
6   knowledge or information, vague goals, confused.

478–9   Introverted or self-conscious or socially insecure, home conflict, nonresponsive or nonverbal, tense, indecisive, lacks knowledge or information, vague goals, confused.

478–X   Lacks skills with the opposite sex, home conflict, mother conflict, sibling conflict, nonresponsive or nonverbal, tense, indecisive, unhappy, worries a great deal, insomnia, lacks knowledge or information, vague goals, confused, poor rapport. Note: Scale 4 coded high was infrequently associated with lack of skills with the opposite sex.

479–0   Home conflict, father conflict, one interview only, lacks knowledge or information, aggressive or belligerent, defensive. This pattern was infrequently associated with shyness in the interview, being nonresponsive or nonverbal, being nonverbal or a nonrelator, indecisiveness.

479–1   Home conflict, defensive, nonresponsive or nonverbal. Note: Scale 9 coded high was infrequently associated with being nonresponsive or nonverbal.

479–2   Home conflict, defensive, aggressive or belligerent.

479–3/5   Home conflict, defensive.

479–6   Introverted or self-conscious or socially insecure, home conflict, defensive, rationalizes a great deal.

479–8   Home conflict, defensive.

479–X   Lacks skills with the opposite sex, home conflict, mother conflict, sibling conflict, nonresponsive or nonverbal, tense, indecisive, unhappy, worries a great deal, insomnia, confused, poor rapport, defensive. Note: Scale 9 coded high was infrequently associated with indecisiveness, being nonresponsive or nonverbal, worrying a great deal, lack of skills with the opposite sex.

48–0   Father conflict, lacks knowledge or information, aggressive or belligerent.

48–9   Introverted or self-conscious or socially insecure.

48–X   Indecisive, unhappy, worries a great deal, insomnia, confused.

489–0   Father conflict, lacks knowledge or information, lacks academic motivation, aggressive or belligerent. This pattern was infrequently associated with introversion or self-consciousness or social insecurity, shyness in the interview, being nonresponsive or nonverbal, being nonverbal or a nonrelator, indecisiveness.

489–2   Aggressive or belligerent.

489–6   Rationalizes a great deal.

489–X   Indecisive, unhappy, worries a great deal, insomnia, confused. Note: Scale 9 coded high was infrequently associated with indecisiveness and worrying a great deal.

49–0   Father conflict, aggressive or belligerent. This pattern was infrequently associated with introversion or self-consciousness or social insecurity,

	shyness in the interview, being nonresponsive or nonverbal, being nonverbal or a nonrelator, indecisiveness.
49–2	Aggressive or belligerent.
49–6	Rationalizes a great deal.
5–0	This pattern was infrequently associated with introversion or self-consciousness or social insecurity, lack of skills with the opposite sex, being nonresponsive or nonverbal, tension.
5–1	Restless.
5–X	Home conflict, insomnia.
56–0	This pattern was infrequently associated with introversion or self-consciousness or social insecurity, lack of skills with the opposite sex, being nonresponsive or a nonrelator, tension.
56–1	Restless.
56–X	Home conflict, insomnia.
567–0	Home conflict, one interview only, wants reassurance only, lacks knowledge or information. This pattern was infrequently associated with introversion or self-consciousness or social insecurity, lack of skills with the opposite sex, being nonresponsive or nonverbal, tension.
567–1	Home conflict, wants reassurance only, nonresponsive or nonverbal, restless.
567–2/3/4/8/ 9	Home conflict, wants reassurance only.
567–X	Lacks skills with the opposite sex, home conflict, mother conflict, sibling conflict, wants reassurance only, nonresponsive or nonverbal, tense, indecisive, unhappy, worries a great deal, insomnia, confused. Note: Scale 5 coded high was infrequently associated with tension.
568–0	Home conflict, aggressive or belligerent, lacks knowledge or information. This pattern was infrequently associated with introversion or self-consciousness or social insecurity, lack of skills with the opposite sex, being nonresponsive or nonverbal, tension.
568–1	Home conflict, restless.
568–2/3/4/7	Home conflict.
568–9	Home conflict, introverted or self-conscious or socially insecure.
568–X	Home conflict, indecisive, unhappy, worries a great deal, insomnia, confused.
569–0	Mother conflict, poor rapport, aggressive or belligerent. Note: Scale 0 coded low was infrequently associated with poor rapport. This pattern was infrequently associated with introversion or self-consciousness or social insecurity, shyness in the interview, lack of skills with the opposite sex, being nonresponsive or nonverbal, being nonverbal or a nonrelator, tension, indecisiveness.
569–1	Mother conflict, poor rapport, restless.
569–2/3/4/7/ 8	Mother conflict, poor rapport.
569–X	Home conflict, mother conflict, poor rapport, insomnia.
57–0	Home conflict, one interview only, wants reassurance only, lacks knowledge or information. This pattern was infrequently associated with introversion or self-consciousness or social insecurity, lack of skills with the opposite sex, being nonresponsive or nonverbal, tension.

CODEBOOK OF MMPI PATTERNS

57–1   Home conflict, wants reassurance only, nonresponsive or nonverbal, restless.

57–2/3/4/6/   Home conflict, wants reassurance only.
    8/9

57–X   Lacks skills with the opposite sex, home conflict, mother conflict, sibling conflict, wants reassurance only, nonresponsive or nonverbal, tense, indecisive, unhappy, worries a great deal, insomnia, confused. Note: Scale 5 coded high was infrequently associated with tension.

578–0   Introverted or self-conscious or socially insecure (78), home conflict, one interview only, wants reassurance only, nonresponsive or nonverbal (78), tense (78), indecisive (78), lacks knowledge or information, vague goals, confused, aggressive or belligerent. Note: Scale 0 coded low was infrequently associated with indecisiveness. This pattern was infrequently associated with introversion or self-consciousness or social insecurity (5–0), lack of skills with the opposite sex, being nonresponsive or nonverbal (5–0), tension (5–0).

578–1/2/3/4/   Introverted or self-conscious or socially insecure, home conflict, wants
    6/9   reassurance only, nonresponsive or nonverbal, tense, indecisive, lacks knowledge or information, vague goals, confused. Note: Scale 5 coded high was infrequently associated with tension.

578–X   Introverted or self-conscious or socially insecure, lacks skills with the opposite sex, home conflict, mother conflict, sibling conflict, wants reassurance only, nonresponsive or nonverbal, tense, indecisive, unhappy, worries a great deal, insomnia, lacks knowledge or information, vague goals, confused. Note: Scale 5 coded high was infrequently associated with tension.

579–0   Home conflict, mother conflict, one interview only, wants reassurance only, lacks knowledge or information, defensive, aggressive or belligerent, poor rapport. Note: Scale 0 coded low was infrequently associated with poor rapport. This pattern was infrequently associated with introversion or self-consciousness or social insecurity, shyness in the interview, lack of skills with the opposite sex, being nonresponsive or nonverbal, being nonverbal or a nonrelator, tension, indecisiveness.

579–1   Home conflict, mother conflict, wants reassurance only, nonresponsive or nonverbal, restless, poor rapport, defensive.

579–2/3/4   Home conflict, mother conflict, wants reassurance only, poor rapport, defensive.

579–6   Home conflict, mother conflict, wants reassurance only, poor rapport, rationalizes a great deal, defensive.

579–8   Home conflict, mother conflict, wants reassurance only, poor rapport, defensive.

579–X   Lacks skills with the opposite sex, home conflict, mother conflict, sibling conflict, wants reassurance only, nonresponsive or nonverbal, tense, indecisive, unhappy, worries a great deal, insomnia, confused, poor rapport, defensive. Note: Scale 5 coded high was infrequently associated with tension.

58–0   Home conflict, lacks knowledge or information, aggressive or belligerent. This pattern was infrequently associated with introversion or self-consciousness or social insecurity, lack of skills with the opposite sex, being nonresponsive or nonverbal, tension.

58–1   Home conflict, restless.

58–2/3/4/6/7   Home conflict.

58–9   Introverted or self-conscious or socially insecure, home conflict.

58–X   Home conflict, indecisive, unhappy, worries a great deal, insomnia, confused.

589–0   Home conflict, mother conflict, lacks knowledge or information, poor rapport, aggressive or belligerent. Note: Scale 0 coded low was infrequently associated with poor rapport. This pattern was infrequently associated with introversion or self-consciousness or social insecurity, shyness in the interview, lack of skills with the opposite sex, being nonresponsive or nonverbal, being nonverbal or a nonrelator, tension, indecisiveness. The 89–0 coding is related to lack of academic motivation and poor academic performance; however, Scale 5 coded high with this pattern suppresses its effect on academic performance and leads to a higher grade distribution than would be expected from the base rate (see reference 5).

589–1   Home conflict, mother conflict, poor rapport, restless.

589–2/3/4   Home conflict, mother conflict, poor rapport.

589–6   Home conflict, mother conflict, poor rapport, rationalizes a great deal.

589–7   Home conflict, mother conflict, poor rapport.

589–X   Home conflict, mother conflict, indecisive, unhappy, worries a great deal, insomnia, confused, poor rapport. Note: Scale 9 coded high was infrequently associated with indecisiveness and worrying a great deal.

59–0   Mother conflict, poor rapport, aggressive or belligerent. Note: Scale 0 coded low was infrequently associated with poor rapport. This pattern was infrequently associated with introversion or self-consciousness or social insecurity, shyness in the interview, lack of skills with the opposite sex, being nonresponsive or nonverbal, being nonverbal or a nonrelator, tension, indecisiveness.

59–1   Mother conflict, poor rapport, restless.

59–2/3/4   Mother conflict, poor rapport.

59–6   Mother conflict, poor rapport, rationalizes a great deal.

59–7/8   Mother conflict, poor rapport.

59–X   Home conflict, mother conflict, poor rapport, insomnia.

67–0   One interview only, lacks knowledge or information.

67–1   Nonresponsive or nonverbal.

67–X   Lacks skills with the opposite sex, home conflict, mother conflict, sibling conflict, nonresponsive or nonverbal, tense, indecisive, unhappy, worries a great deal, insomnia, confused.

678–0   Introverted or self-conscious or socially insecure, one interview only, nonresponsive or nonverbal, tense, indecisive, lacks knowledge or information, vague goals, confused, aggressive or belligerent. Note: Scale 0 coded low was infrequently associated with introversion or self-consciousness or social insecurity, being nonresponsive or nonverbal, indecisiveness.

678–1/2/3/4/   Introverted or self-conscious or socially insecure, nonresponsive or non-
    5/9   verbal, tense, indecisive, lacks knowledge or information, vague goals, confused.

678–X   Introverted or self-conscious or socially insecure, lacks skills with the opposite sex, mother conflict, sibling conflict, nonresponsive or non-verbal, tense, indecisive, unhappy, worries a great deal, insomnia, lacks knowledge or information, vague goals, confused.

679–0   Home conflict, one interview only, lacks knowledge or information, aggressive or belligerent, defensive. This pattern was infrequently associated with introversion or self-consciousness or social insecurity, shyness in the interview, being nonresponsive or nonverbal, being non-verbal or a nonrelator, indecisiveness.

679–1   Home conflict, defensive, nonresponsive or nonverbal.

679–2/3/4/5/   Home conflict, defensive.
    8

679–X   Lacks skills with the opposite sex, home conflict, mother conflict, sibling conflict, nonresponsive or nonverbal, tense, indecisive, unhappy, worries a great deal, insomnia, confused, defensive. Note: Scale 9 coded high was infrequently associated with being nonresponsive or nonverbal, indecisiveness, worrying a great deal, lack of skills with the opposite sex.

68–0   Lacks knowledge or information, aggressive or belligerent.

68–9   Introverted or self-conscious or socially insecure.

68–X   Indecisive, unhappy, worries a great deal, insomnia, confused.

689–0   Lacks knowledge or information, aggressive or belligerent, lacks academic motivation. This pattern was infrequently associated with introversion or self-consciousness or social insecurity, shyness in the interview, being nonresponsive or nonverbal, being nonverbal or a nonrelator, indecisiveness.

689–X   Indecisive, unhappy, worries a great deal, insomnia, confused. Note: Scale 9 coded high was infrequently associated with indecisiveness and worrying a great deal.

69–0   Aggressive or belligerent. This pattern was infrequently associated with introversion or self-consciousness or social insecurity, shyness in the interview, being nonresponsive or nonverbal, being nonverbal or a nonrelator, indecisiveness.

7–0   One interview only, lacks knowledge or information.

7–1   Nonresponsive or nonverbal.

7–X   Lacks skills with the opposite sex, mother conflict, sibling conflict, non-responsive or nonverbal, tense, indecisive, unhappy, worries a great deal, insomnia, confused.

78–0   Introverted or self-conscious or socially insecure, one interview only, nonresponsive or nonverbal, tense, indecisive, lacks knowledge or information, vague goals, confused, aggressive or belligerent. Note: Scale 0 coded low was infrequently associated with introversion or self-consciousness or social insecurity, being nonresponsive or nonverbal, indecisiveness.

78–1/2/3/4/   Introverted or self-conscious or socially insecure, nonresponsive or non-
    5/6/9   verbal, tense, indecisive, lacks knowledge or information, vague goals, confused.

78–X	Introverted or self-conscious or socially insecure, lacks skills with the opposite sex, mother conflict, sibling conflict, nonresponsive or nonverbal, tense, indecisive, unhappy, worries a great deal, insomnia, lacks knowledge or information, vague goals, confused.
789–0	Introverted or self-conscious or socially insecure (78), home conflict, one interview only, nonresponsive or nonverbal (78), tense, indecisive (78), lacks knowledge or information, vague goals, confused, lacks academic motivation, aggressive or belligerent, defensive. This pattern was infrequently associated with introversion (9–0), shyness in the interview, being nonresponsive or nonverbal (9–0), being nonverbal or a nonrelator, indecisiveness (9–0).
789–1/2/3/4/ 5	Introverted or self-conscious or socially insecure, home conflict, nonresponsive or nonverbal, tense, indecisive, lacks knowledge or information, vague goals, confused, defensive. Note: Scale 9 coded high was infrequently associated with being nonresponsive or nonverbal and indecisiveness.
789–6	Introverted or self-conscious or socially insecure, home conflict, nonresponsive or nonverbal, tense, indecisive, lacks knowledge or information, vague goals, confused, rationalizes a great deal, defensive. Note· Scale 9 coded high was infrequently associated with being nonresponsive or nonverbal and indecisiveness.
789–X	Introverted or self-conscious or socially insecure, lacks skills with the opposite sex, home conflict, mother conflict, sibling conflict, nonresponsive or nonverbal, tense, indecisive, unhappy, worries a great deal, insomnia, lacks knowledge or information, vague goals, confused, defensive. Note: Scale 9 coded high was infrequently associated with being nonresponsive or nonverbal, indecisiveness, worrying a great deal, lack of skills with the opposite sex.
79–0	Home conflict, defensive, aggressive or belligerent, lacks knowledge or information, one interview only. This pattern was infrequently associated with introversion or self-consciousness or social insecurity, shyness in the interview, being nonresponsive or nonverbal, being nonverbal or a nonrelator, indecisiveness.
79–1/2/3/4/ 5	Home conflict, defensive.
79–6	Home conflict, defensive, rationalizes a great deal.
79–8	Home conflict, defensive.
79–X	Lacks skills with the opposite sex, home conflict, mother conflict, sibling conflict, nonresponsive or nonverbal, tense, indecisive, unhappy, worries a great deal, insomnia, confused, defensive. Note: Scale 9 coded high was infrequently associated with being nonresponsive or nonverbal, indecisiveness, worrying a great deal, lack of skills with the opposite sex.
8–0	Lacks knowledge or information, aggressive or belligerent.
8–9	Introverted or self-conscious or socially insecure.
8–X	Indecisive, unhappy, worries a great deal, insomnia, confused.
89–0	Lacks knowledge or information, lacks academic motivation, aggressive or belligerent. This pattern was infrequently associated with introversion or self-consciousness or social insecurity, shyness in the interview, being

	nonresponsive or nonverbal, being nonverbal or a nonrelator, indecisiveness.
89–6	Rationalizes a great deal.
89–X	Indecisive, unhappy, worries a great deal, insomnia, confused. Note: Scale 9 coded high was infrequently associated with indecisiveness and worrying a great deal.
9–0	Aggressive or belligerent. This pattern was infrequently associated with introversion or self-consciousness or social insecurity, shyness in the interview, being nonresponsive or nonverbal, being nonverbal or a nonrelator, indecisiveness.
9–6	Rationalizes a great deal.

0–1	Lacks skills with the opposite sex.
0–3	Socially insecure.
0–5	Socially shy, shy in the interview.
0–9	Socially shy.
0–X	Socially shy, lacks skills with the opposite sex, nonverbal.
01–3	Socially insecure.
01–5	Socially shy, shy in the interview, headaches.
01–9	Socially shy.
01–X	Socially shy, lacks skills with the opposite sex, nonverbal.
012–3	Socially shy, lacks skills with the opposite sex, socially insecure, lacks self-confidence.
012–4	Socially shy, lacks skills with the opposite sex, lacks self-confidence.
012–5	Socially shy, lacks skills with the opposite sex, shy in the interview, socially insecure, lacks self-confidence, indecisive, depressed, anxieties, nervous, headaches, tense on examinations, wants answers.
012–6	Socially shy, lacks skills with the opposite sex, socially insecure, lacks self-confidence, nonverbal.
012–7/8	Socially shy, lacks skills with the opposite sex, lacks self-confidence.
012–9	Socially shy, lacks skills with the opposite sex, lacks self-confidence, mother conflict.
012–X	Socially shy, lacks skills with the opposite sex, lacks self-confidence, nonverbal, depressed.
013–2	Socially extroverted (3–2).
013–5	Socially shy, shy in the interview, insomnia, exhaustion, headaches, home conflict, distractible in study.
013–9	Socially shy.
013–X	Socially shy, lacks skills with the opposite sex, father conflict, mother conflict, tense on examinations, verbal (3–X), nonverbal (0–X).
014–2	Father conflict (04), socially extroverted (4–2). Note: Scale 2 coded low was infrequently associated with father conflict.
014–3	Socially insecure (0–3), father conflict. Note: Scale 4 coded high was infrequently associated with social insecurity.
014–5	Socially shy, lacks skills with the opposite sex, shy in the interview (0–5), father conflict, rebellious toward home, anxieties, headaches, indecisive. Note: Scale 4 coded high was infrequently associated with shyness in the interview.
014–6	Father conflict, vague goals, lacks academic drive.

73

014–7/8	Father conflict.
014–9	Father conflict, socially shy.
014–X	Father conflict, socially shy, lacks skills with the opposite sex, nonverbal.
015–3	Socially insecure.
015–9	Socially shy (0–9). Note: Scale 5 coded high was infrequently associated with social shyness.
015–X	Socially shy (0–X), lacks skills with the opposite sex, nonverbal, distractible in study. Note: Scale 5 coded high was infrequently associated with social shyness.
016–2	Socially shy (06), socially extroverted (6–2), physical inferiority.
016–3	Socially shy, socially insecure, physical inferiority.
016–4	Socially shy, shy in the interview, physical inferiority.
016–5	Socially shy, shy in the interview, physical inferiority, headaches.
016–7/8/9	Socially shy, physical inferiority.
016–X	Socially shy, lacks skills with the opposite sex, physical inferiority, nonverbal, 8+ conferences, restless.
017–2	Socially shy (07), socially insecure (07), lacks self-confidence (07). Note: Scale 2 coded low was infrequently associated with social shyness, social insecurity, lack of self-confidence.
017–3	Socially shy, socially insecure, lacks self-confidence, cried in the interview.
017–4	Socially shy, socially insecure, lacks self-confidence.
017–5	Socially shy, socially insecure, shy in the interview, lacks self-confidence, indecisive, anxieties, nervous, exhaustion, insomnia, headaches.
017–6/8/9	Socially shy, socially insecure, lacks self-confidence.
017–X	Socially shy, socially insecure, lacks skills with the opposite sex, lacks self-confidence, sibling conflict, nonverbal, headaches.
018–2	Socially shy (08), shy in the interview, nonverbal, nervous. Note: Scale 2 coded low was infrequently associated with social shyness.
018–3	Socially shy, shy in the interview, socially insecure, nonverbal, nervous.
018–4	Socially shy, shy in the interview, nonverbal, nervous.
018–5	Socially shy, shy in the interview, nonverbal, nervous, anxieties, headaches, distractible in study.
018–6/7/9	Socially shy, shy in the interview, nonverbal, nervous.
018–X	Socially shy, shy in the interview, lacks skills with the opposite sex, nonverbal, 8+ conferences, nervous, depressed, mother conflict, father conflict, sibling conflict.
019–2	Socially shy (09), socially extroverted (9–2). Note: Scale 2 coded low was infrequently associated with social shyness.
019–3	Socially shy, socially insecure, vague goals.
019–4	Socially shy, shy in the interview (9–4), nonresponsive. Note: Scale 9 coded high was infrequently associated with shyness in the interview.
019–5	Socially shy, shy in the interview (0–5), verbal, exhaustion, headaches. Note: Scale 9 coded high was infrequently associated with shyness in the interview.
019–6/7/8	Socially shy.
019–X	Socially shy, lacks skills with the opposite sex, nonverbal.
02–1	Socially shy, lacks skills with the opposite sex, lacks self-confidence, physical inferiority.

FEMALE SECTION

02–3	Socially shy, lacks skills with the opposite sex, socially insecure, lacks self-confidence.
02–4	Socially shy, lacks skills with the opposite sex, lacks self-confidence.
02–5	Socially shy, lacks skills with the opposite sex, shy in the interview, socially insecure, depressed, anxieties, nervous, wants answers, lacks self-confidence, indecisive, tense on examinations.
02–6	Socially shy, lacks skills with the opposite sex, socially insecure, lacks self-confidence, nonverbal.
02–7/8	Socially shy, lacks skills with the opposite sex, lacks self-confidence.
02–9	Socially shy, lacks skills with the opposite sex, lacks self-confidence, mother conflict.
02–X	Socially shy, lacks skills with the opposite sex, lacks self-confidence, nonverbal, depressed.
023–1	Socially shy, lacks skills with the opposite sex, lacks self-confidence, physical inferiority.
023–4	Socially shy, lacks skills with the opposite sex, lacks self-confidence.
023–5	Socially shy, lacks skills with the opposite sex, shy in the interview, socially insecure, lacks self-confidence, indecisive, depressed, exhaustion, nervous, anxious, insomnia, headaches, tense on examinations, distractible in study, home conflict, wants answers.
023–6	Socially shy, lacks skills with the opposite sex, socially insecure, lacks self-confidence, nonverbal.
023–7/8	Socially shy, lacks skills with the opposite sex, lacks self-confidence.
023–9	Socially shy, lacks skills with the opposite sex, lacks self-confidence, mother conflict.
023–X	Socially shy, lacks skills with the opposite sex, lacks self-confidence, mother conflict, father conflict, tense on examinations, nonverbal (0–X), verbal (3–X), depressed.
024–1	Socially shy (02), lacks skills with the opposite sex (02, 24, 0–1), social extroversion (4–1), lacks self-confidence, indecisive, physical inferiority, father conflict, depressed, anxieties.
024–3	Socially shy, lacks skills with the opposite sex, socially insecure (0–3), lacks self-confidence, indecisive, father conflict, depressed, anxieties. Note: Scale 4 coded high was infrequently associated with social insecurity.
024–5	Socially shy, lacks skills with the opposite sex, socially insecure (2–5), shy in the interview (0–5), lacks self-confidence, indecisive, father conflict, rebellious toward home, mother conflict, depressed, anxieties, nervous, tense on examinations, wants answers. Note: Scale 4 coded high was infrequently associated with social insecurity and shyness in the interview.
024–6	Socially shy, lacks skills with the opposite sex, socially insecure (2–6), lacks self-confidence, indecisive, father conflict, depressed, exhaustion, vague goals, nonverbal. Note: Scale 4 coded high was infrequently associated with social insecurity.
024–7/8	Socially shy, lacks skills with the opposite sex, lacks self-confidence, indecisive, father conflict, depressed, anxieties.
024–9	Socially shy, lacks skills with the opposite sex, lacks self-confidence, indecisive, father conflict, mother conflict, depressed, anxieties.

024–X   Socially shy, lacks skills with the opposite sex, lacks self-confidence, indecisive, father conflict, mother conflict, depressed, anxieties, nonverbal.

025–1   Socially shy, lacks skills with the opposite sex, lacks self-confidence, physical inferiority. Note: Scale 5 coded high was infrequently associated with social shyness.

025–3   Socially shy, lacks skills with the opposite sex, socially insecure, lacks self-confidence. Note: Scale 5 coded high was infrequently associated with social shyness.

025–4   Socially shy, lacks skills with the opposite sex, lacks self-confidence. Note: Scale 5 coded high was infrequently associated with social shyness.

025–6   Socially shy (02), lacks skills with the opposite sex, socially insecure, lacks self-confidence, nonverbal. Note: Scale 5 coded high was infrequently associated with social shyness.

025–7/8   Socially shy (02), lacks skills with the opposite sex, lacks self-confidence. Note: Scale 5 coded high was infrequently associated with social shyness.

025–9   Socially shy, lacks skills with the opposite sex, lacks self-confidence, mother conflict. Note: Scale 5 coded high was infrequently associated with social shyness.

025–X   Socially shy, lacks skills with the opposite sex, lacks self-confidence, depressed, nonverbal, distractible in study. Note: Scale 5 coded high was infrequently associated with social shyness.

026–1   Socially shy, lacks skills with the opposite sex, lacks self-confidence, physical inferiority, 8+ conferences, anxieties.

026–3   Socially shy, lacks skills with the opposite sex, socially insecure, lacks self-confidence, physical inferiority, anxieties, 8+ conferences.

026–4   Socially shy, lacks skills with the opposite sex, shy in the interview, lacks self-confidence, physical inferiority, anxieties, 8+ conferences.

026–5   Socially shy, lacks skills with the opposite sex, shy in the interview, socially insecure, lacks self-confidence, physical inferiority, indecisive, depressed, anxieties, nervous, tense on examinations, nonresponsive, wants answers, 8+ conferences.

026–7/8   Socially shy, lacks skills with the opposite sex, lacks self-confidence, physical inferiority, anxieties, 8+ conferences.

026–9   Socially shy, lacks skills with the opposite sex, lacks self-confidence, physical inferiority, anxieties, 8+ conferences, mother conflict.

026–X   Socially shy, lacks skills with the opposite sex, lacks self-confidence, physical inferiority, depressed, anxieties, restless, 8+ conferences, nonverbal.

027–1   Socially shy, lacks skills with the opposite sex, socially insecure, lacks self-confidence, physical inferiority, depressed, anxieties, 4 to 7 conferences, distractible in study.

027–3   Socially shy, lacks skills with the opposite sex, socially insecure, lacks self-confidence, depressed, anxieties, 4 to 7 conferences, cried in the interview, distractible in study.

027–4   Socially shy, lacks skills with the opposite sex, socially insecure, lacks self-confidence, depressed, anxieties, 4 to 7 conferences, distractible in study.

027–5	Socially shy, lacks skills with the opposite sex, socially insecure, shy in the interview, lacks self-confidence, indecisive, depressed, anxieties, 4 to 7 conferences, wants answers, distractible in study, tense on examinations, insomnia, exhaustion, nervous, headaches.
027–6	Socially shy, lacks skills with the opposite sex, socially insecure, lacks self-confidence, depressed, anxieties, 4 to 7 conferences, nonverbal, distractible in study.
027–8	Socially shy, lacks skills with the opposite sex, socially insecure, lacks self-confidence, depressed, anxieties, 4 to 7 conferences, distractible in study.
027–9	Socially shy, lacks skills with the opposite sex, socially insecure, lacks self-confidence, depressed, anxieties, 4 to 7 conferences, distractible in study, mother conflict.
027–X	Socially shy, lacks skills with the opposite sex, socially insecure, lacks self-confidence, depressed, anxieties, headaches, 4 to 7 conferences, nonverbal, distractible in study, sibling conflict.
028–1	Socially shy, lacks skills with the opposite sex, socially insecure, lacks self-confidence, physical inferiority, depressed, anxieties, nervous, nonverbal, distractible in study.
028–3	Socially shy, lacks skills with the opposite sex, socially insecure, shy in the interview, lacks self-confidence, depressed, anxieties, nervous, nonverbal, distractible in study.
028–4	Socially shy, lacks skills with the opposite sex, shy in the interview, lacks self-confidence, depressed, anxieties, nervous, nonverbal, distractible in study.
028–5	Socially shy, lacks skills with the opposite sex, socially insecure, shy in the interview, lacks self-confidence, indecisive, depressed, anxieties, nervous, nonverbal, wants answers, distractible in study, tense on examinations.
028–6	Socially shy, lacks skills with the opposite sex, socially insecure, shy in the interview, lacks self-confidence, depressed, anxieties, nervous, nonverbal, distractible in study.
028–7	Socially shy, lacks skills with the opposite sex, shy in the interview, lacks self-confidence, depressed, anxieties, nervous, nonverbal, distractible in study.
028–9	Socially shy, lacks skills with the opposite sex, socially insecure, lacks self-confidence, depressed, anxieties, nervous, nonverbal, distractible in study, mother conflict.
028–X	Socially shy, lacks skills with the opposite sex, socially insecure, lacks self-confidence, depressed, anxieties, nervous, nonverbal, 8+ conferences, distractible in study, mother conflict, father conflict, sibling conflict.
029–1	Socially shy (09, 02, 09–1), lacks skills with the opposite sex, socially insecure (29), socially extroverted (9–1), lacks self-confidence, physical inferiority, vague goals.
029–3	Socially shy, lacks skills with the opposite sex, socially insecure, lacks self-confidence, vague goals.
029–4	Socially shy, lacks skills with the opposite sex, socially insecure, shy in the interview (9–4), lacks self-confidence, nonresponsive. Note:

Scale 9 coded high was infrequently associated with shyness in the interview.

029–5   Socially shy, lacks skills with the opposite sex, socially insecure, shy in the interview (0–5), lacks self-confidence, indecisive, depressed, anxieties, nervous, exhaustion, verbal, wants answers, tense on examinations. Note: Scale 9 coded high was infrequently associated with shyness in the interview.

029–6   Socially shy, lacks skills with the opposite sex, socially insecure, lacks self-confidence, nonverbal.

029–7/8   Socially shy, lacks skills with the opposite sex, socially insecure, lacks self-confidence.

029–X   Socially shy, lacks skills with the opposite sex, socially insecure, lacks self-confidence, nonverbal, depressed.

03–1   Lacks skills with the opposite sex.

03–2   Socially extroverted (3–2).

03–5   Socially shy, shy in the interview, exhaustion, insomnia, headaches, home conflict, distractible in study.

03–9   Socially shy.

03–X   Socially shy, lacks skills with the opposite sex, nonverbal (0–X), verbal (3–X), father conflict, mother conflict, tense on examinations.

034–1   Lacks skills with the opposite sex, socially extroverted (4–1), father conflict, home conflict, lacks academic drive.

034–2   Socially extroverted, father conflict (04), family conflict (34), lacks academic drive. Note: Scale 2 coded low was infrequently associated with father or family conflict.

034–5   Socially shy, lacks skills with the opposite sex, shy in the interview (0–5), father conflict, home conflict, rebellious toward home, anxieties, exhaustion, insomnia, headaches, lacks academic drive, distractible in study, indecisive. Scale 4 coded high was infrequently associated with shyness in the interview.

034–6   Father conflict, home conflict, lacks academic drive, vague goals.

034–7/8   Father conflict, home conflict, lacks academic drive.

034–9   Socially shy, father conflict, home conflict, lacks academic drive.

034–X   Socially shy, lacks skills with the opposite sex, father conflict, home conflict, mother conflict, lacks academic drive, nonverbal (0–X), verbal (3–X), tense on examinations.

035–1   Lacks skills with the opposite sex.

035–2   Socially extroverted (3–2).

035–9   Socially shy (0–9). Note: Scale 5 coded high was infrequently associated with social shyness.

035–X   Socially shy (0–X), lacks skills with the opposite sex, father conflict (3–X), mother conflict, nonverbal (0–X), verbal (3–X), tense on examinations, distractible in study. Note: Scale 5 coded high was infrequently associated with social shyness and father conflict.

036–1   Socially shy, lacks skills with the opposite sex, physical inferiority.

036–2   Socially shy (06), social extroversion (3–2), physical inferiority. Note: Scale 2 coded low was infrequently associated with social shyness.

036–4   Socially shy, shy in the interview, physical inferiority.

FEMALE SECTION

036–5	Socially shy, shy in the interview, exhaustion, insomnia, headaches, home conflict, physical inferiority, distractible in study.
036–9	Socially shy, physical inferiority.
036–X	Socially shy, lacks skills with the opposite sex, physical inferiority, father conflict, mother conflict, nonverbal (0–X), verbal (3–X), 8+ conferences, restless, tense on examinations.
037–1	Socially shy, socially insecure, lacks skills with the opposite sex, anxieties, insomnia, lacks self-confidence.
037–2	Socially shy (07), socially insecure (07), socially extroverted (3–2), anxieties, insomnia, lacks self-confidence (07). Note: Scale 2 coded low was infrequently associated with social shyness, social insecurity, lack of self-confidence.
037–4	Socially shy, socially insecure, anxieties, insomnia, lacks self-confidence.
037–5	Socially shy, socially insecure, shy in the interview, anxieties, insomnia, exhaustion, nervous, headaches, lacks self-confidence, indecisive, home conflict, distractible in study.
037–6/8/9	Socially shy, socially insecure, anxieties, insomnia, lacks self-confidence.
037–X	Socially shy, socially insecure, lacks skills with the opposite sex, anxieties, insomnia, headaches, lacks self-confidence, father conflict, mother conflict, sibling conflict, tense on examinations, nonverbal (0–X), verbal (3–X).
038–1	Socially shy, lacks skills with the opposite sex, shy in the interview, nonverbal (08), verbal (38), nervous.
038–2	Socially shy (08), shy in the interview, socially extroverted (3–2), nonverbal (08), verbal (38), nervous. Note: Scale 2 coded low was infrequently associated with social shyness.
038–4	Socially shy, shy in the interview, nonverbal (08), verbal (38), nervous.
038–5	Socially shy, shy in the interview, nonverbal (08, 08–5), verbal (38, 38–5), anxious, nervous, exhaustion, insomnia, headaches, home conflict, distractible in study.
038–6/7/9	Socially shy, shy in the interview, nonverbal (08), verbal (38), nervous.
038–X	Socially shy, shy in the interview, lacks skills with the opposite sex, nonverbal (08, 0–X), verbal (38, 3–X), 8+ conferences, nervous, depressed, father conflict, mother conflict, sibling conflict, tense on examinations.
039–1	Socially shy (09), lacks skills with the opposite sex, socially extroverted (39, 9–1), vague goals, marriage oriented.
039–2	Socially shy (09), socially extroverted (39, 9–2, 3–2), marriage oriented. Note: Scale 2 coded low was infrequently associated with social shyness.
039–4	Socially shy (09), shy in the interview (9–4), socially extroverted (39), marriage oriented, nonresponsive (9–4). Note: Scale 3 coded high was infrequently associated with nonresponsiveness.
039–5	Socially shy (09, 0–5), shy in the interview (0–5), socially extroverted (39), marriage oriented, distractible in study, exhaustion, insomnia, headaches, home conflict, verbal.
039–6/7/8	Socially shy (09), socially extroverted (39), marriage oriented.
039–X	Socially shy (09, 0–X), lacks skills with the opposite sex, socially extroverted (39), marriage oriented.

CODEBOOK OF MMPI PATTERNS

04–1   Lacks skills with the opposite sex, socially extroverted (4–1), father conflict.

04–2   Socially extroverted (4–2), father conflict. Note: Scale 2 coded low was infrequently associated with father conflict.

04–3   Socially insecure, father conflict. Note: Scale 4 coded high was infrequently associated with social insecurity.

04–5   Socially shy, lacks skills with the opposite sex, shy in the interview, father conflict, rebellious toward home, indecisive, anxieties. Note: Scale 4 coded high was infrequently associated with shyness in the interview.

04–6   Father conflict, vague goals.

04–7/8   Father conflict.

04–9   Father conflict, socially shy.

04–X   Father conflict, socially shy, lacks skills with the opposite sex, nonverbal.

045–1   Father conflict, lacks skills with the opposite sex, socially extroverted. Note: Scale 5 coded high was infrequently associated with father conflict.

045–2   Father conflict, socially extroverted (4–2). Note: Scale 5 coded high was infrequently associated with father conflict.

045–3   Father conflict, socially insecure. Note: Scale 4 coded high was infrequently associated with social insecurity; Scale 5 coded high was infrequently associated with father conflict.

045–6/7/8   Father conflict, vague goals. Note: Scale 5 coded high was infrequently associated with father conflict.

045–9   Father conflict, socially shy. Note: Scale 5 coded high was infrequently associated with father conflict.

045–X   Father conflict, socially shy, lacks skills with the opposite sex, nonverbal, distractible in study. Note: Scale 5 coded high was infrequently associated with social shyness; Scale 5 coded high was infrequently associated with father conflict.

046–1   Socially shy (06), lacks skills with the opposite sex, socially extroverted (4–1), father conflict, physical inferiority.

046–2   Socially shy (06), socially extroverted (4–2, 6–2), father conflict, physical inferiority. Note: Scale 2 coded low was infrequently associated with social shyness or father conflict.

046–3   Socially shy, socially insecure, father conflict, physical inferiority. Note: Scale 4 coded high was infrequently associated with social insecurity.

046–5   Socially shy, shy in the interview, lacks skills with the opposite sex, father conflict, rebellious toward home, physical inferiority, indecisive, anxieties. Note: Scale 4 coded high was infrequently associated with shyness in the interview.

046–7/8/9   Socially shy, father conflict, physical inferiority.

046–X   Socially shy, lacks skills with the opposite sex, father conflict, nonverbal, 8+ conferences, restless.

047–1   Socially shy (07), socially insecure (07), lacks skills with the opposite sex, socially extroverted (4–1), father conflict, rebellious toward home, lacks self-confidence, insomnia. Note: Scale 4 coded high was infrequently associated with social insecurity.

047–2   Socially shy (07), socially insecure (07), socially extroverted (4–2), father conflict, rebellious toward home, lacks self-confidence. Note: Scale 2 coded low was infrequently associated with social shyness, father conflict, lack of self-confidence; Scale 4 coded high was infrequently associated with social insecurity.

047–3 Socially shy, socially insecure, father conflict, rebellious toward home, lacks self-confidence, insomnia, cried in the interview. Note: Scale 4 coded high was infrequently associated with social insecurity.

047–5 Socially shy, socially insecure, shy in the interview, lacks skills with the opposite sex, father conflict, rebellious toward home, anxieties, insomnia, exhaustion, nervous, headaches, indecisive, lacks self-confidence. Note: Scale 4 coded high was infrequently associated with social insecurity.

047–6 Socially shy, socially insecure, father conflict, rebellious toward home, insomnia, vague goals, lacks self-confidence. Note: Scale 4 coded high was infrequently associated with social insecurity.

047–8/9 Socially shy, socially insecure, father conflict, rebellious toward home, insomnia, lacks self-confidence. Note: Scale 4 coded high was infrequently associated with social insecurity.

047–X Socially shy, socially insecure, lacks skills with the opposite sex, father conflict, rebellious toward home, sibling conflict, insomnia, headaches, nonverbal, tense on examinations, lacks self-confidence. Note: Scale 4 coded high was infrequently associated with social insecurity.

048–1 Socially shy (08), shy in the interview (08), lacks skills with the opposite sex, socially extroverted (4–1), father conflict, overprotective mother, depressed, insomnia, nervous, nonverbal. Note: Scale 4 coded high was infrequently associated with shyness in the interview.

048–2 Socially shy (08), shy in the interview (08), socially extroverted (4–2), father conflict, overprotective mother, depressed (48), insomnia, nervous, nonverbal. Note: Scale 2 coded low was infrequently associated with social shyness and father conflict; Scale 4 coded high was infrequently associated with shyness in the interview.

048–3 Socially shy, socially insecure, shy in the interview, father conflict, overprotective mother, depressed, insomnia, nervous, nonverbal. Note: Scale 4 coded high was infrequently associated with shyness in the interview.

048–5 Socially shy, shy in the interview, lacks skills with the opposite sex, father conflict, overprotective mother, rebellious toward home, depressed, insomnia, nervous, anxieties, distractible in study, nonverbal, indecisive. Note: Scale 4 coded high was infrequently associated with shyness in the interview.

048–6 Socially shy, shy in the interview, father conflict, overprotective mother, depressed, insomnia, nervous, vague goals, nonverbal. Note: Scale 4 coded high was infrequently associated with shyness in the interview.

048–7/9 Socially shy, shy in the interview, father conflict, overprotective mother, depressed, insomnia, nervous, nonverbal. Note: Scale 4 coded high was infrequently associated with shyness in the interview.

048–X Socially shy, shy in the interview, lacks skills with the opposite sex, father conflict, overprotective mother, mother conflict, sibling conflict, depressed, insomnia, headaches, nervous, 8+ conferences, nonverbal.

Note: Scale 4 coded high was infrequently associated with shyness in the interview.

049–1   Socially shy (09, 09–1), lacks skills with the opposite sex, socially extroverted (49, 4–1), father conflict, home conflict, vague goals, verbal.

049–2   Socially shy (09), socially extroverted (49, 4–2), father conflict, family conflict, vague goals, verbal. Note: Scale 2 coded low was infrequently associated with social shyness, father conflict, family conflict.

049–3   Socially shy (09), socially insecure (0–3), socially extroverted (49), father conflict, family conflict, vague goals, verbal. Note: Scale 4 coded high was infrequently associated with social insecurity.

049–5   Socially shy (09, 0–5), shy in the interview (0–5), lacks skills with the opposite sex, socially extroverted (49), father conflict, family conflict, rebellious toward home, vague goals, verbal (49, 9–5), indecisive, anxieties, exhaustion.

049–6/7/8   Socially shy (09), socially extroverted (49), father conflict, family conflict, vague goals, verbal.

049–X   Socially shy (09, 0–X), lacks skills with the opposite sex, socially extroverted (49), father conflict, family conflict, vague goals, verbal (49), non-verbal (0–X).

05–1   Lacks skills with the opposite sex.

05–3   Socially insecure.

05–9   Socially shy. Note: Scale 5 coded high was infrequently associated with social shyness.

05–X   Socially shy, lacks skills with the opposite sex, nonverbal, distractible in study. Note: Scale 5 coded high was infrequently associated with social shyness.

056–1   Socially shy, lacks skills with the opposite sex, physical inferiority. Note: Scale 5 coded high was infrequently associated with social shyness.

056–2   Socially shy (06), socially extroverted (6–2), physical inferiority. Note: Scale 2 coded low was infrequently associated with social shyness; Scale 5 coded high was infrequently associated with social shyness.

056–3   Socially shy, socially insecure, physical inferiority. Note: Scale 5 coded high was infrequently associated with social shyness.

056–4   Socially shy, shy in the interview, physical inferiority. Note: Scale 5 coded high was infrequently associated with social shyness.

056–7/8/9   Socially shy, physical inferiority. Note: Scale 5 coded high was infrequently associated with social shyness.

056–X   Socially shy, lacks skills with the opposite sex, physical inferiority, nonverbal, 8+ conferences, restless, distractible in study. Note: Scale 5 coded high was infrequently associated with 8+ conferences and social shyness.

057–1   Socially shy, socially insecure, lacks skills with the opposite sex, lacks self-confidence. Note: Scale 5 coded high was infrequently associated with social shyness.

057–2   Socially shy, socially insecure, lacks self-confidence. Note: Scale 2 coded low was infrequently associated with social shyness and lack of self-confidence; Scale 5 coded high was infrequently associated with social shyness.

057–3   Socially shy, socially insecure, lacks self-confidence, cried in the inter-

	view. Note: Scale 5 coded high was infrequently associated with social shyness.
057–4/6/8/9	Socially shy, socially insecure, lacks self-confidence. Note: Scale 5 coded high was infrequently associated with social shyness.
057–X	Socially shy, socially insecure, lacks skills with the opposite sex, lacks self-confidence, nonverbal, sibling conflict, headaches, distractible in study. Note: Scale 5 coded high was infrequently associated with headaches and social shyness.
058–1	Socially shy, shy in the interview, lacks skills with the opposite sex, nonverbal, nervous. Note: Scale 5 coded high was infrequently associated with social shyness.
058–2	Socially shy, shy in the interview, nonverbal, nervous. Note: Scale 2 coded low was infrequently associated with social shyness; Scale 5 coded high was infrequently associated with social shyness.
058–3	Socially shy, shy in the interview, socially insecure, nonverbal, nervous. Note: Scale 5 coded high was infrequently associated with social shyness.
058–4/6/7/9	Socially shy, shy in the interview, nonverbal, nervous. Note: Scale 5 coded high was infrequently associated with social shyness.
058–X	Socially shy, shy in the interview, lacks skills with the opposite sex, nonverbal, 8+ conferences, depressed, nervous, father conflict, mother conflict, sibling conflict, distractible in study. Note: Scale 5 coded high was infrequently associated with social shyness.
059–1	Socially shy (09), socially extroverted (59, 9–1), lacks skills with the opposite sex, vague goals. Note: Scale 5 coded high was infrequently associated with social shyness.
059–2	Socially shy (09), socially extroverted (59, 9–2), vague goals. Note: Scale 2 coded low was infrequently associated with social shyness; Scale 5 coded high was infrequently associated with social shyness.
059–3	Socially shy (09), socially insecure (0–3), socially extroverted (59), vague goals. Note: Scale 5 coded high was infrequently associated with social shyness.
059–4	Socially shy (09), shy in the interview, socially extroverted (59), vague goals, nonresponsive. Note: Scale 9 coded high was infrequently associated with shyness in the interview; Scale 5 coded high was infrequently associated with social shyness.
059–6/7/8	Socially shy (09), socially extroverted (59), vague goals. Note: Scale 5 coded high was infrequently associated with social shyness.
059–X	Socially shy (09), socially extroverted (59), lacks skills with the opposite sex, vague goals, distractible in study, nonverbal. Note: Scale 5 coded high was infrequently associated with social shyness.
06–1	Socially shy, lacks skills with the opposite sex, physical inferiority.
06–2	Socially shy (06), socially extroverted (6–2), physical inferiority. Note: Scale 2 coded low was infrequently associated with social shyness.
06–3/4/5	Socially shy, socially insecure, physical inferiority.
06–7/8/9	Socially shy, physical inferiority.
06–X	Socially shy, lacks skills with the opposite sex, physical inferiority, nonverbal, 8+ conferences, restless.

067–1   Socially shy, socially insecure, lacks skills with the opposite sex, physical inferiority, lacks self-confidence.

067–2   Socially shy (06, 07), socially insecure (07), socially extroverted (6–2), physical inferiority, lacks self-confidence. Note: Scale 2 coded low was infrequently associated with social shyness, social insecurity, lack of self-confidence.

067–3   Socially shy, socially insecure, physical inferiority, lacks self-confidence, cried in the interview.

067–4   Socially shy, socially insecure, shy in the interview, physical inferiority, lacks self-confidence.

067–5   Socially shy, socially insecure, shy in the interview, physical inferiority, lacks self-confidence, indecisive, anxieties, nervous, exhaustion, insomnia, headaches.

067–8/9   Socially shy, socially insecure, physical inferiority, lacks self-confidence.

067–X   Socially shy, socially insecure, lacks skills with the opposite sex, physical inferiority, lacks self-confidence, restless, headaches, sibling conflict, nonverbal, 8+ conferences.

068–1   Socially shy, shy in the interview, lacks skills with the opposite sex, physical inferiority, nonverbal, 8+ conferences, nervous.

068–2   Socially shy (06, 08), shy in the interview, socially extroverted (6–2), physical inferiority, nonverbal, 8+ conferences, nervous. Note: Scale 2 coded low was infrequently associated with social shyness.

068–3   Socially shy, shy in the interview, socially insecure, physical inferiority, nonverbal, 8+ conferences, nervous.

068–4   Socially shy, shy in the interview, physical inferiority, nonverbal, 8+ conferences, nervous.

068–5   Socially shy, shy in the interview, physical inferiority, nonverbal, 8+ conferences, anxieties, nervous, distractible in study.

068–7/9   Socially shy, shy in the interview, physical inferiority, nonverbal, 8+ conferences, nervous.

068–X   Socially shy, shy in the interview, lacks skills with the opposite sex, physical inferiority, nonverbal, 8+ conferences, depressed, restless, nervous, father conflict, mother conflict, sibling conflict.

069–1   Socially shy (06, 09), socially extroverted (9–1), lacks skills with the opposite sex, physical inferiority, vague goals.

069–2   Socially shy (06, 09), socially extroverted (9–2, 6–2), physical inferiority. Note: Scale 2 coded low was infrequently associated with social shyness.

069–3   Socially shy, socially insecure, physical inferiority, vague goals.

069–4   Socially shy, shy in the interview, physical inferiority, nonresponsive. Note: Scale 9 coded high was infrequently associated with shyness in the interview.

069–5   Socially shy, shy in the interview, physical inferiority, verbal, exhaustion. Note: Scale 9 coded high was infrequently associated with shyness in the interview.

069–7/8   Socially shy, physical inferiority.

069–X   Socially shy, lacks skills with the opposite sex, physical inferiority, nonverbal, 8+ conferences, restless.

FEMALE SECTION

07–1 Socially shy, socially insecure, lacks skills with the opposite sex, lacks self-confidence.

07–2 Socially shy, socially insecure, lacks self-confidence. Note: Scale 2 coded low was infrequently associated with social shyness, social insecurity, lack of self-confidence.

07–3 Socially shy, socially insecure, lacks self-confidence, cried in the interview.

07–4 Socially shy, socially insecure, lacks self-confidence.

07–5 Socially shy, socially insecure, shy in the interview, lacks self-confidence, indecisive, anxieties, exhaustion, nervous, insomnia, headaches.

07–6/8/9 Socially shy, socially insecure, lacks self-confidence.

07–X Socially shy, socially insecure, lacks skills with the opposite sex, lacks self-confidence, sibling conflict, nonverbal, headaches.

078–1 Socially shy, socially insecure, shy in the interview, lacks skills with the opposite sex, lacks self-confidence, nonverbal, nervous, insomnia.

078–2 Socially shy, socially insecure, shy in the interview, lacks skills with the opposite sex, lacks self-confidence, nonverbal, nervous, insomnia. Note: Scale 2 coded low was infrequently associated with social shyness, social insecurity, lack of self-confidence.

078–3 Socially shy, socially insecure, shy in the interview, lacks self-confidence, nonverbal, cried in the interview, nervous, insomnia.

078–4 Socially shy, socially insecure, shy in the interview, lacks self-confidence, nonverbal, nervous, insomnia.

078–5 Socially shy, socially insecure, shy in the interview, lacks self-confidence, indecisive, nonverbal, anxieties, nervous, insomnia, exhaustion, headaches, distractible in study.

078–6/9 Socially shy, socially insecure, shy in the interview, lacks self-confidence, nonverbal, nervous, insomnia.

078–X Socially shy, socially insecure, shy in the interview, lacks skills with the opposite sex, lacks self-confidence, nonverbal, 8+ conferences, nervous, insomnia, exhaustion, depressed, headaches, father conflict, mother conflict, sibling conflict.

079–1 Socially shy (07, 09), socially insecure (07), lacks skills with the opposite sex, socially extroverted (9–1), lacks self-confidence, confused, sibling conflict, nervous, distractible in study, vague goals.

079–2 Socially shy (07, 09), socially insecure (07), socially extroverted (9–2), lacks self-confidence, confused, sibling conflict, nervous, distractible in study. Note: Scale 2 coded low was infrequently associated with social shyness, social insecurity, lack of self-confidence.

079–3 Socially shy, socially insecure, lacks self-confidence, sibling conflict, nervous, distractible in study, vague goals, cried in the interview.

079–4 Socially shy, socially insecure, shy in the interview, lacks self-confidence, confused, sibling conflict, nervous, distractible in study, nonresponsive. Note: Scale 9 coded high was infrequently associated with shyness in the interview.

079–5 Socially shy, socially insecure, shy in the interview, lacks self-confidence, confused, indecisive, sibling conflict, nervous, exhaustion, insomnia, headaches, anxieties, verbal, distractible in study. Note: Scale 9 coded high was infrequently associated with shyness in the interview.

85

CODEBOOK OF MMPI PATTERNS

079–6/8   Socially shy, socially insecure, lacks self-confidence, confused, sibling conflict, nervous, distractible in study.

079–X   Socially shy, socially insecure, lacks skills with the opposite sex, lacks self-confidence, confused, sibling conflict, nervous, headaches, distractible in study, nonverbal.

08–1   Socially shy, shy in the interview, lacks skills with the opposite sex, nonverbal, nervous.

08–2   Socially shy, shy in the interview, lacks skills with the opposite sex, nonverbal, nervous. Note: Scale 2 coded low was infrequently associated with social shyness.

08–3   Socially shy, shy in the interview, socially insecure, nonverbal, nervous.

08–4   Socially shy, shy in the interview, nonverbal, nervous.

08–5   Socially shy, shy in the interview, nonverbal, nervous, anxieties, distractible in study.

08–6/7/9   Socially shy, shy in the interview, nonverbal, nervous.

08–X   Socially shy, shy in the interview, lacks skills with the opposite sex, nonverbal, 8+ conferences, nervous, depressed, father conflict, mother conflict, sibling conflict.

089–1   Socially shy (09, 08), shy in the interview, lacks skills with the opposite sex, socially extroverted (9–1), nervous, restless, nonverbal (08), verbal (89), 8+ conferences, resistant in the interview, confused, vague goals. Note: Scale 9 coded high was infrequently associated with shyness in the interview.

089–2   Socially shy (09, 08), shy in the interview, socially extroverted (9–2), nervous, restless, exhaustion, nonverbal (08), verbal (89), 8+ conferences, resistant in the interview, confused. Note: Scale 2 coded low was infrequently associated with social shyness and confusion; Scale 9 coded high was infrequently associated with shyness in the interview.

089–3   Socially shy, shy in the interview, socially insecure, nervous, restless, nonverbal (08), verbal (89), 8+ conferences, resistant in the interview, confused, vague goals. Note: Scale 9 coded high was infrequently associated with shyness in the interview.

089–4   Socially shy, shy in the interview, nervous, restless, nonverbal (08), verbal (89), 8+ conferences, resistant in the interview, nonresponsive, confused. Note: Scale 9 coded high was infrequently associated with shyness in the interview.

089–5   Socially shy, shy in the interview, nervous, restless, anxieties, exhaustion, nonverbal (08, 08–5), verbal (89, 89–5, 9–5), 8+ conferences, resistant in the interview, wants answers, confused, distractible in study. Note: Scale 5 coded low was infrequently associated with resistance in the interview; Scale 9 coded high was infrequently associated with shyness in the interview.

089–6/7   Socially shy, shy in the interview, nervous, restless, nonverbal (08), verbal (89), 8+ conferences, resistant in the interview, confused. Note: Scale 9 coded high was infrequently associated with shyness in the interview.

089–X   Socially shy, shy in the interview, lacks skills with the opposite sex, nervous, restless, depressed, nonverbal (08, 0–X), verbal (89), 8+ conferences, resistant in the interview, confused, father conflict, mother

FEMALE SECTION

	conflict, sibling conflict. Note: Scale 9 coded high was infrequently associated with shyness in the interview.
1–5	Headaches.
12–0	Tense on examinations.
12–4	Lacks self-confidence.
12–5	Anxieties, depressed, headaches, nervous, indecisive, tense on examinations, wants answers, socially shy, socially insecure, lacks skills with the opposite sex.
12–6	Nonverbal, lacks self-confidence, socially insecure.
12–9	Mother conflict.
12–X	Depressed, lacks skills with the opposite sex.
123–0	Tense on examinations, marriage oriented, lacks academic drive, socially extroverted.
123–4	Lacks self-confidence.
123–5	Headaches, depressed, anxieties, exhaustion, insomnia, nervous, home conflict, wants answers, indecisive, distractible in study, tense on examinations, socially shy, lacks skills with the opposite sex, socially insecure. Note: Scale 3 coded high was infrequently associated with social insecurity.
123–6	Lacks self-confidence, nonverbal, socially insecure. Note: Scale 3 coded high was infrequently associated with social insecurity.
123–9	Mother conflict.
123–X	Mother conflict, father conflict, depressed, verbal, tense on examinations, lacks skills with the opposite sex.
124–0	Anxieties, depressed, father conflict, indecisive, lacks skills with the opposite sex, socially extroverted, tense on examinations, lacks academic drive. Note: Scale 0 coded low was infrequently associated with depression and lack of skills with the opposite sex.
124–3	Anxieties, depressed, father conflict, indecisive, lacks skills with the opposite sex.
124–5	Anxieties, depressed, headaches, nervous, father conflict, mother conflict, rebellious toward home, indecisive, lacks skills with the opposite sex, socially shy, socially insecure, tense on examinations, wants answers. Note: Scale 4 coded high was infrequently associated with social insecurity.
124–6	Anxieties, depressed, father conflict, indecisive, lacks self-confidence, nonverbal, vague goals, lacks skills with the opposite sex, socially insecure. Note: Scale 4 coded high was infrequently associated with social insecurity.
124–7/8	Anxieties, depressed, father conflict, indecisive, lacks skills with the opposite sex.
124–9	Anxieties, depressed, father conflict, mother conflict, indecisive, lacks skills with the opposite sex.
124–X	Anxieties, depressed, father conflict, indecisive, lacks skills with the opposite sex.
125–0	Tense on examinations, socially extroverted.
125–4	Lacks self-confidence.
125–6	Lacks self-confidence, nonverbal, socially insecure.
125–9	Mother conflict.

125–X	Depressed, distractible in study, lacks skills with the opposite sex. Note: Scale 5 coded high was infrequently associated with depression.
126–0	Anxieties, resistant in the interview, 8+ conferences, tense on examinations, socially extroverted.
126–3	Anxieties, 8+ conferences.
126–4	Anxieties, 8+ conferences, shy in the interview, lacks self-confidence.
126–5	Anxieties, depressed, nervous, headaches, nonresponsive, wants answers, 8+ conferences, physical inferiority, indecisive, tense on examinations, socially shy, socially insecure, lacks skills with the opposite sex.
126–7/8	Anxieties, 8+ conferences.
126–9	Anxieties, 8+ conferences, mother conflict.
126–X	Anxieties, depressed, restless, 8+ conferences, lacks skills with the opposite sex.
127–0	Anxieties, depressed, socially insecure, socially shy, distractible in study, tense on examinations, lacks self-confidence, 4 to 7 conferences. Note: Scale 0 coded low was infrequently associated with depression, social insecurity, social shyness.
127–3	Anxieties, depressed, socially insecure, socially shy, distractible in study, lacks self-confidence, 4 to 7 conferences, cried in the interview.
127–4	Anxieties, depressed, socially insecure, socially shy, distractible in study, lacks self-confidence, 4 to 7 conferences.
127–5	Anxieties, depressed, nervous, exhaustion, headaches, insomnia, distractible in study, tense on examinations, lacks self-confidence, indecisive, 4 to 7 conferences, wants answers, socially insecure, socially shy, lacks skills with the opposite sex.
127–6	Anxieties, depressed, distractible in study, lacks self-confidence, 4 to 7 conferences, nonverbal, socially insecure, socially shy.
127–8	Anxieties, depressed, distractible in study, lacks self-confidence, 4 to 7 conferences, socially insecure, socially shy.
127–9	Anxieties, depressed, distractible in study, lacks self-confidence, 4 to 7 conferences, socially insecure, socially shy, mother conflict.
127–X	Anxieties, depressed, headaches, distractible in study, lacks self-confidence, 4 to 7 conferences, socially insecure, socially shy, lacks skills with the opposite sex, sibling conflict.
128–0	Anxieties, depressed, distractible in study, tense on examinations, verbal, lacks skills with the opposite sex. Note: Scale 0 coded low was infrequently associated with depression and lack of skills with the opposite sex.
128–3	Anxieties, depressed, distractible in study, lacks skills with the opposite sex.
128–4	Anxieties, depressed, distractible in study, lacks skills with the opposite sex, lacks self-confidence.
128–5	Anxieties, depressed, headaches, nervous, distractible in study, tense on examinations, lacks skills with the opposite sex, socially shy, socially insecure, wants answers, indecisive.
128–6	Anxieties, depressed, distractible in study, lacks skills with the opposite sex, socially insecure, lacks self-confidence, nonverbal.
128–7	Anxieties, depressed, distractible in study, lacks skills with the opposite sex.

FEMALE SECTION

128–9	Anxieties, depressed, distractible in study, lacks skills with the opposite sex, mother conflict.
128–X	Anxieties, depressed, distractible in study, lacks skills with the opposite sex, father conflict, mother conflict, sibling conflict, 8+ conferences.
129–0	Lacks self-confidence, socially insecure (29), socially extroverted (9–0), tense on examinations, marriage oriented, verbal. Note: Scale 0 coded low was infrequently associated with social insecurity.
129–3	Lacks self-confidence, socially insecure, vague goals.
129–4	Lacks self-confidence, socially insecure, shy in the interview, nonresponsive. Note: Scale 9 coded high was infrequently associated with shyness in the interview.
129–5	Lacks self-confidence, indecisive, socially insecure, socially shy, lacks skills with the opposite sex, anxieties, nervous, depressed, exhaustion, headaches, tense on examinations, verbal, wants answers.
129–6	Lacks self-confidence, socially insecure, nonverbal.
129–7/8	Lacks self-confidence, socially insecure.
129–X	Lacks self-confidence, socially insecure, lacks skills with the opposite sex, depressed.
13–0	Lacks academic drive, marriage oriented, tense on examinations, socially extroverted.
13–2	Socially extroverted.
13–5	Exhaustion, insomnia, headaches, distractible in study, home conflict.
13–X	Mother conflict, father conflict, tense on examinations, verbal.
134–0	Lacks academic drive, tense on examinations, marriage oriented, home conflict, socially extroverted. Note: Scale 0 coded low was infrequently associated with home conflict.
134–2	Lacks academic drive, home conflict, socially extroverted. Note: Scale 2 coded low was infrequently associated with home conflict.
134–5	Lacks academic drive, distractible in study, home conflict, rebellious toward home, anxieties, exhaustion, insomnia, headaches, indecisive, lacks skills with the opposite sex.
134–6	Lacks academic drive, vague goals, home conflict.
134–7/8/9	Lacks academic drive, home conflict.
134–X	Lacks academic drive, tense on examinations, home conflict, father conflict, mother conflict, verbal.
135–0	Lacks academic drive, marriage oriented, tense on examinations, socially extroverted.
135–2	Socially extroverted.
135–X	Mother conflict, father conflict, distractible in study, tense on examinations, verbal. Note: Scale 5 coded high was infrequently associated with father conflict.
136–0	Lacks academic drive, tense on examinations, marriage oriented, socially extroverted, resistant in the interview.
136–2	Socially extroverted.
136–4	Shy in the interview.
136–5	Exhaustion, insomnia, headaches, physical inferiority, distractible in study, family conflict.
136–X	Mother conflict, father conflict, verbal, 8+ conferences, restless, tense on examinations.

137–0	Anxieties, insomnia, lacks academic drive, marriage oriented, tense on examinations, socially extroverted.
137–2	Anxieties, insomnia, socially extroverted.
137–4	Anxieties, insomnia.
137–5	Anxieties, insomnia, exhaustion, nervous, headaches, lacks self-confidence, indecisive, distractible in study, family conflict, socially insecure. Note: Scale 3 coded high was infrequently associated with social insecurity.
137–6/8/9	Anxieties, insomnia.
137–X	Anxieties, insomnia, headaches, father conflict, mother conflict, sibling conflict, tense on examinations, verbal.
138–0	Verbal, lacks academic drive, marriage oriented, tense on examinations, socially extroverted.
138–2	Verbal, socially extroverted.
138–4	Verbal.
138–5	Verbal, anxieties, exhaustion, insomnia, headaches, distractible in study, home conflict.
138–6/7/9	Verbal.
138–X	Verbal, 8+ conferences, depressed, father conflict, mother conflict, sibling conflict, tense on examinations, lacks skills with the opposite sex.
139–0	Marriage oriented, tense on examinations, lacks academic drive, socially extroverted, verbal.
139–2	Marriage oriented, socially extroverted.
139–4	Marriage oriented, socially extroverted, shy in the interview, nonresponsive. Note: Scale 3 coded high was infrequently associated with nonresponsiveness.
139–5	Marriage oriented, distractible in study, socially extroverted, exhaustion, insomnia, headaches, home conflict, verbal.
139–6/7/8	Marriage oriented, socially extroverted.
139–X	Marriage oriented, tense on examinations, socially extroverted, father conflict, mother conflict, verbal.
14–0	Lacks academic drive, socially extroverted.
14–2	Socially extroverted.
14–5	Anxieties, headaches, rebellious toward home, indecisive, lacks skills with the opposite sex.
14–6	Vague goals.
145–0	Lacks academic drive, socially extroverted.
145–2	Socially extroverted.
145–6	Vague goals.
145–X	Distractible in study.
146–0	Lacks academic drive, socially extroverted, resistant in the interview.
146–2	Socially extroverted.
146–5	Physical inferiority, indecisive, anxieties, headaches, lacks skills with the opposite sex, rebellious toward home.
146–X	Restless, 8+ conferences.
147–0	Insomnia, rebellious toward home, lacks academic drive, socially extroverted.
147–2	Insomnia, rebellious toward home, socially extroverted.
147–3	Insomnia, rebellious toward home, cried in the interview.

147–5	Insomnia, headaches, exhaustion, nervous, anxieties, rebellious toward home, indecisive, socially insecure, lacks skills with the opposite sex, lacks self-confidence. Note: Scale 4 coded high was infrequently associated with social insecurity.
147–6	Insomnia, rebellious toward home, vague goals.
147–8/9	Insomnia, rebellious toward home.
147–X	Insomnia, headaches, rebellious toward home, sibling conflict, tense on examinations.
148–0	Insomnia, depressed, overprotective mother, verbal, lacks academic drive, socially extroverted. Note: Scale 0 coded low was infrequently associated with depression.
148–2	Insomnia, depressed, overprotective mother, socially extroverted.
148–3	Insomnia, depressed, overprotective mother.
148–5	Insomnia, depressed, anxieties, headaches, overprotective mother, rebellious toward home, distractible in study, lacks skills with the opposite sex, indecisive.
148–6	Insomnia, depressed, overprotective mother, vague goals.
148–7/9	Insomnia, depressed, overprotective mother.
148–X	Insomnia, depressed, headaches, overprotective mother, mother conflict, father conflict, sibling conflict, 8+ conferences, lacks skills with the opposite sex.
149–0	Socially extroverted, vague goals, marriage oriented, lacks academic drive, verbal, home conflict. Note: Scale 0 coded low was infrequently associated with home conflict.
149–2	Socially extroverted, vague goals, verbal, home conflict. Note: Scale 2 coded low was infrequently associated with home conflict.
149–3	Socially extroverted, vague goals, verbal, home conflict.
149–5	Socially extroverted, vague goals, verbal, home conflict, exhaustion, headaches, anxieties, rebellious toward home, indecisive.
149–6/7/8/X	Socially extroverted, vague goals, verbal, home conflict.
15–0	Socially extroverted.
15–X	Distractible in study.
156–0	Socially extroverted, resistant in the interview.
156–2	Socially extroverted.
156–4	Shy in the interview.
156–X	Distractible in study, restless, 8+ conferences. Note: Scale 5 coded high was infrequently associated with 8+ conferences.
157–0	Socially extroverted.
157–3	Cried in the interview.
157–X	Distractible in study, sibling conflict, headaches. Note: Scale 5 coded high was infrequently associated with headaches.
158–0	Socially extroverted, verbal.
158–X	Distractible in study, father conflict, mother conflict, sibling conflict, 8+ conferences, lacks skills with the opposite sex. Note: Scale 5 coded high was infrequently associated with father conflict, 8+ conferences.
159–0	Socially extroverted, vague goals, marriage oriented, verbal.
159–2/3	Socially extroverted, vague goals.
159–4	Socially extroverted, shy in the interview, vague goals, nonresponsive.
159–6/7/8	Socially extroverted, vague goals.

159–X	Socially extroverted, vague goals, distractible in study.
16–0	Socially extroverted, resistant in the interview.
16–2	Socially extroverted.
16–4	Shy in the interview.
16–5	Socially extroverted, headaches.
16–X	Restless, 8+ conferences.
167–0	Socially extroverted, resistant in the interview.
167–2	Socially extroverted.
167–3	Cried in the interview.
167–4	Shy in the interview.
167–5	Anxieties, nervous, exhaustion, insomnia, headaches, indecisive, physical inferiority, lacks self-confidence, socially insecure.
167–X	Restless, headaches, 8+ conferences, sibling conflict.
168–0	Socially extroverted, verbal, resistant in the interview, 8+ conferences.
168–2	Socially extroverted, 8+ conferences.
168–3	8+ conferences.
168–4	Shy in the interview, 8+ conferences.
168–5	8+ conferences, anxieties, headaches, physical inferiority, distractible in study.
168–7/9	8+ conferences.
168–X	8+ conferences, depressed, restless, father conflict, mother conflict, sibling conflict, lacks skills with the opposite sex.
169–0	Socially extroverted, marriage oriented, resistant in the interview, verbal.
169–2	Socially extroverted.
169–3	Vague goals.
169–4	Shy in the interview, nonresponsive. Note: Scale 9 coded high was infrequently associated with shyness in the interview.
169–5	Socially extroverted, exhaustion, headaches, verbal.
169–X	8+ conferences, restless.
17–3	Cried in the interview.
17–5	Anxieties, nervous, exhaustion, insomnia, headaches, lacks self-confidence, indecisive, socially insecure.
17–X	Headaches, sibling conflict.
178–0	Nervous, insomnia, lacks self-confidence, verbal.
178–2	Nervous, insomnia, lacks self-confidence. Note: Scale 2 coded low was infrequently associated with lack of self-confidence.
178–3	Nervous, insomnia, lacks self-confidence, cried in the interview.
178–5	Nervous, insomnia, headaches, anxieties, exhaustion, lacks self-confidence, indecisive, distractible in study, socially insecure.
178–6/9	Nervous, insomnia, lacks self-confidence.
178–X	Nervous, insomnia, headaches, exhaustion, depressed, lacks self-confidence, 8+ conferences, father conflict, mother conflict, sibling conflict, lacks skills with the opposite sex.
179–0	Confused, nervous, exhaustion, distractible in study, marriage oriented, sibling conflict, verbal, socially extroverted. Note: Scale 0 coded low was infrequently associated with confusion, exhaustion, sibling conflict.
179–2	Confused, nervous, distractible in study, sibling conflict, extroverted. Note: Scale 2 coded low was infrequently associated with confusion.

FEMALE SECTION

179–3	Confused, nervous, distractible in study, vague goals, sibling conflict, cried in the interview.
179–4	Confused, nervous, distractible in study, sibling conflict, shy in the interview, nonresponsive. Note: Scale 9 coded high was infrequently associated with shyness in the interview.
179–5	Confused, indecisive, lacks self-confidence, distractible in study, nervous, anxieties, insomnia, headaches, exhaustion, sibling conflict, verbal, socially insecure.
179–6/8	Confused, nervous, distractible in study, sibling conflict.
179–X	Confused, nervous, headaches, distractible in study, sibling conflict.
18–0	Verbal.
18–5	Anxieties, headaches, distractible in study.
18–X	Depressed, father conflict, mother conflict, sibling conflict, 8+ conferences, lacks skills with the opposite sex.
189–0	Confused, restless, verbal, 8+ conferences, resistant in the interview, marriage oriented, socially extroverted. Note: Scale 0 coded low was infrequently associated with confusion.
189–2	Confused, restless, exhaustion, verbal, 8+ conferences, resistant in the interview, socially extroverted. Note: Scale 2 coded low was infrequently associated with confusion.
189–3	Confused, restless, verbal, 8+ conferences, resistant in the interview, vague goals.
189–4	Confused, restless, verbal, 8+ conferences, resistant in the interview, nonresponsive, shy in the interview.
189–5	Confused, restless, anxieties, exhaustion, headaches, verbal, 8+ conferences, resistant in the interview, wants answers, distractible in study. Note: Scale 5 coded low was infrequently associated with resistance in the interview.
189–6	Confused, restless, verbal, 8+ conferences, resistant in the interview.
189–7	Confused, restless, verbal, 8+ conferences, resistant in the interview.
189–X	Confused, restless, depressed, verbal, 8+ conferences, resistant in the interview, father conflict, mother conflict, sibling conflict, lacks skills with the opposite sex.
19–0	Marriage oriented, socially extroverted, verbal.
19–2	Socially extroverted.
19–3	Vague goals.
19–4	Shy in the interview, nonresponsive. Note: Scale 9 coded high was infrequently associated with shyness in the interview.
19–5	Exhaustion, headaches, verbal.
2–0	Tense on examinations.
2–1	Lacks self-confidence, physical inferiority.
2–4	Lacks self-confidence.
2–5	Anxieties, nervous, depressed, indecisive, wants answers, tense on examinations, socially shy, lacks skills with the opposite sex, socially insecure.
2–6	Lacks self-confidence, nonverbal, socially insecure.
2–9	Mother conflict.
2–X	Depressed, lacks skills with the opposite sex.
23–0	Lacks academic drive, marriage oriented, tense on examinations, socially extroverted.

23–1	Lacks self-confidence, physical inferiority.
23–4	Lacks self-confidence.
23–5	Anxieties, nervous, depressed, insomnia, exhaustion, headaches, distractible in study, tense on examinations, indecisive, home conflict, wants answers, socially insecure, socially shy, lacks skills with the opposite sex. Note: Scale 3 coded high was infrequently associated with social insecurity.
23–6	Lacks self-confidence, nonverbal, socially insecure. Note: Scale 3 coded high was infrequently associated with social insecurity.
23–9	Mother conflict.
23–X	Mother conflict, father conflict, verbal, tense on examinations, lacks skills with the opposite sex, depressed.
234–0	Father conflict, home conflict, lacks academic drive, marriage oriented, tense on examinations, depressed, anxieties, indecisive, lacks skills with the opposite sex, socially extroverted. Note: Scale 0 coded low was infrequently associated with home conflict, depression, lack of skills with the opposite sex.
234–1	Father conflict, home conflict, lacks academic drive, depressed, anxieties, indecisive, lacks self-confidence, physical inferiority, lacks skills with the opposite sex, socially extroverted.
234–5	Father conflict, home conflict, mother conflict, rebellious toward home, lacks academic drive, tense on examinations, distractible in study, depressed, anxieties, nervous, exhaustion, insomnia, headaches, indecisive, lacks skills with the opposite sex, socially insecure, socially shy, wants answers. Note: Scale 4 coded high was infrequently associated with social insecurity.
234–6	Father conflict, home conflict, lacks academic drive, vague goals, depressed, anxieties, indecisive, lacks self-confidence, lacks skills with the opposite sex, socially insecure, nonverbal. Note: Scale 4 coded high was infrequently associated with social insecurity.
234–7/8	Father conflict, home conflict, lacks academic drive, depressed, anxieties, indecisive, lacks skills with the opposite sex.
234–9	Father conflict, home conflict, mother conflict, lacks academic drive, depressed, anxieties, indecisive, lacks skills with the opposite sex.
234–X	Father conflict, home conflict, mother conflict, lacks academic drive, tense on examinations, depressed, anxieties, indecisive, lacks skills with the opposite sex, verbal.
235–0	Lacks academic drive, tense on examinations, marriage oriented, socially extroverted.
235–1	Socially shy, lacks self-confidence, physical inferiority. Note: Scale 5 coded high was infrequently associated with social shyness.
235–4	Lacks self-confidence.
235–6	Lacks self-confidence, socially insecure, nonverbal. Note: Scale 3 coded high was infrequently associated with social insecurity.
235–9	Mother conflict.
235–X	Mother conflict, father conflict, depressed, tense on examinations, distractible in study, verbal, lacks skills with the opposite sex. Note: Scale 5 coded high was infrequently associated with father conflict.

FEMALE SECTION

236–0	Anxieties, resistant in the interview, 8+ conferences, tense on examinations, marriage oriented, lacks academic drive, socially extroverted.
236–1	Anxieties, 8+ conferences, lacks self-confidence, physical inferiority.
236–4	Anxieties, 8+ conferences, lacks self-confidence, shy in the interview.
236–5	Anxieties, depressed, nervous, exhaustion, insomnia, headaches, 8+ conferences, wants answers, nonresponsive, physical inferiority, indecisive, home conflict, tense on examinations, distractible in study, socially shy, lacks skills with the opposite sex, socially insecure. Note: Scale 3 coded high was infrequently associated with nonresponsiveness.
236–7/8	Anxieties, 8+ conferences.
236–9	Anxieties, 8+ conferences, mother conflict.
236–X	Anxieties, depressed, restless, 8+ conferences, verbal, mother conflict, father conflict, tense on examinations, lacks skills with the opposite sex.
237–0	Anxieties, depressed, insomnia, lacks self-confidence, distractible in study, tense on examinations, marriage oriented, lacks academic drive, socially shy (27), socially insecure (27), socially extroverted (3–0), 4 to 7 conferences. Note: Scale 0 coded low was infrequently associated with depression, lack of self-confidence, social shyness, social insecurity; Scale 3 coded high was infrequently associated with social insecurity.
237–1	Anxieties, depressed, insomnia, lacks self-confidence, physical inferiority, distractible in study, socially shy, socially insecure, 4 to 7 conferences. Note: Scale 3 coded high was infrequently associated with social insecurity.
237–4	Anxieties, depressed, insomnia, lacks self-confidence, distractible in study, socially shy, socially insecure, 4 to 7 conferences. Note: Scale 3 coded high was infrequently associated with social insecurity.
237–5	Anxieties, depressed, insomnia, nervous, headaches, exhaustion, lacks self-confidence, indecisive, distractible in study, tense on examinations, socially shy, socially insecure, lacks skills with the opposite sex, 4 to 7 conferences, wants answers, home conflict. Note: Scale 3 coded high was infrequently associated with social insecurity.
237–6/8	Anxieties, depressed, insomnia, lacks self-confidence, distractible in study, socially shy, socially insecure, 4 to 7 conferences. Note: Scale 3 coded high was infrequently associated with social insecurity.
237–9	Anxieties, depressed, insomnia, lacks self-confidence, distractible in study, socially shy, socially insecure, 4 to 7 conferences, mother conflict. Note: Scale 3 coded high was infrequently associated with social insecurity.
237–X	Anxieties, depressed, insomnia, headaches, lacks self-confidence, distractible in study, tense on examinations, socially shy, socially insecure, lacks skills with the opposite sex, 4 to 7 conferences, verbal, mother conflict, father conflict, sibling conflict. Note: Scale 3 coded high was infrequently associated with social insecurity.
238–0	Anxieties, depressed, verbal, distractible in study, tense on examinations, lacks academic motivation, marriage oriented, lacks skills with the opposite sex, socially extroverted. Note: Scale 0 coded low was infrequently associated with depression and lack of skills with the opposite sex.
238–1	Anxieties, depressed, verbal, distractible in study, lacks skills with the opposite sex, lacks self-confidence, physical inferiority.

238–4   Anxieties, depressed, verbal, distractible in study, lacks skills with the opposite sex, lacks self-confidence.

238–5   Anxieties, depressed, nervous, headaches, insomnia, exhaustion, verbal, wants answers, distractible in study, tense on examinations, lacks skills with the opposite sex, socially shy, socially insecure, indecisive, family conflict.

238–6   Anxieties, depressed, verbal (38), nonverbal (2–6), distractible in study, lacks skills with the opposite sex, socially insecure, lacks self-confidence.

238–7   Anxieties, depressed, verbal, distractible in study, lacks skills with the opposite sex.

238–9   Anxieties, depressed, verbal, distractible in study, lacks skills with the opposite sex, mother conflict.

238–X   Anxieties, depressed, verbal, 8+ conferences, distractible in study, tense on examinations, lacks skills with the opposite sex, mother conflict, father conflict, sibling conflict.

239–0   Lacks self-confidence, marriage oriented, tense on examinations, lacks academic drive, socially insecure (29), socially extroverted (39, 39–0, 3–0, 9–0), verbal. Note: Scale 0 coded low was infrequently associated with lack of self-confidence and social insecurity; Scale 3 coded high was infrequently associated with social insecurity.

239–1   Lacks self-confidence, physical inferiority, marriage oriented, vague goals, socially insecure (29), socially extroverted (39, 9–1). Note: Scale 3 coded high was infrequently associated with social insecurity.

239–4   Lacks self-confidence, marriage oriented, socially insecure (29), socially extroverted (39), shy in the interview, nonresponsive. Note: Scale 3 coded high was infrequently associated with nonresponsiveness and social insecurity.

239–5   Lacks self-confidence, indecisive, marriage oriented, tense on examinations, distractible in study, socially insecure (29, 2–5), socially extroverted (39), socially shy (2–5), lacks skills with the opposite sex, depressed, nervous, anxieties, headaches, insomnia, exhaustion, wants answers, verbal, home conflict. Note: Scale 3 coded high was infrequently associated with social insecurity.

239–6   Lacks self-confidence, marriage oriented, socially insecure (29, 2–6), socially extroverted (39), nonverbal. Note: Scale 3 coded high was infrequently associated with social insecurity.

239–7/8   Lacks self-confidence, marriage oriented, socially insecure (29), socially extroverted (39). Note: Scale 3 coded high was infrequently associated with social insecurity.

239–X   Lacks self-confidence, marriage oriented, tense on examinations, socially insecure (29), socially extroverted (39), lacks skills with the opposite sex, depressed, verbal, father conflict, mother conflict. Note: Scale 3 coded high was infrequently associated with social insecurity.

24–0   Anxieties, depressed, father conflict, indecisive, lacks skills with the opposite sex, socially extroverted, lacks academic drive, tense on examinations. Note: Scale 0 coded low was infrequently associated with depression and lack of skills with the opposite sex.

24–1   Anxieties, depressed, father conflict, indecisive, lacks self-confidence, physical inferiority, lacks skills with the opposite sex, socially extroverted.

24–3   Anxieties, depressed, father conflict, indecisive, lacks skills with the opposite sex.

24–5   Anxieties, depressed, nervous, father conflict, rebellious toward home, mother conflict, indecisive, lacks skills with the opposite sex, socially shy, socially insecure, tense on examinations, wants answers. Note: Scale 4 coded high was infrequently associated with social insecurity.

24–6   Anxieties, depressed, father conflict, indecisive, lacks self-confidence, lacks skills with the opposite sex, socially insecure, vague goals, nonverbal. Note: Scale 4 coded high was infrequently associated with social insecurity.

24–7/8   Anxieties, depressed, father conflict, indecisive, lacks skills with the opposite sex.

24–9   Anxieties, depressed, father conflict, mother conflict, indecisive, lacks skills with the opposite sex.

24–X   Anxieties, depressed, father conflict, indecisive, lacks skills with the opposite sex.

245–0   Anxieties, depressed, father conflict, indecisive, lacks skills with the opposite sex, socially extroverted, tense on examinations, lacks academic drive. Note: Scale 5 coded high was infrequently associated with anxieties, depression, and father conflict; Scale 0 coded low was infrequently associated with depression and lack of skills with the opposite sex.

245–1   Anxieties, depressed, father conflict, indecisive, lacks self-confidence, physical inferiority, lacks skills with the opposite sex, socially extroverted. Note: Scale 5 coded high was infrequently associated with anxieties, depression, father conflict.

245–3   Anxieties, depressed, father conflict, indecisive, lacks skills with the opposite sex. Note: Scale 5 coded high was infrequently associated with anxieties, depression, father conflict.

245–6   Anxieties, depressed, father conflict, indecisive, lacks self-confidence, lacks skills with the opposite sex, socially insecure, vague goals, nonverbal. Note: Scale 4 coded high was infrequently associated with social insecurity; Scale 5 coded high was infrequently associated with anxieties, depression, father conflict.

245–7/8   Anxieties, depressed, father conflict, indecisive, lacks skills with the opposite sex. Note: Scale 5 coded high was infrequently associated with anxieties, depression, father conflict.

245–9   Anxieties, depressed, father conflict, mother conflict, indecisive, lacks skills with the opposite sex. Note: Scale 5 coded high was infrequently associated with anxieties, depression, father conflict.

245–X   Anxieties, depressed, father conflict, indecisive, lacks skills with the opposite sex, distractible in study. Note: Scale 5 coded high was infrequently associated with anxieties, depression, father conflict.

246–0   Anxieties, depressed, indecisive, father conflict, lacks skills with the opposite sex, socially extroverted, resistant in the interview, 8+ conferences, tense on examinations, lacks academic drive. Note: Scale 0 coded low was infrequently associated with depression and lack of skills with the opposite sex.

246–1 Anxieties, depressed, indecisive, lacks self-confidence, physical inferiority, father conflict, lacks skills with the opposite sex, socially extroverted, 8+ conferences.

246–3 Anxieties, depressed, indecisive, father conflict, lacks skills with the opposite sex, 8+ conferences.

246–5 Anxieties, depressed, nervous, indecisive, physical inferiority, father conflict, mother conflict, rebellious toward home, lacks skills with the opposite sex, socially shy, socially insecure, 8+ conferences, wants answers, nonresponsive, tense on examinations. Note: Scale 4 coded high was infrequently associated with social insecurity.

246–7/8 Anxieties, depressed, indecisive, father conflict, lacks skills with the opposite sex, 8+ conferences.

246–9 Anxieties, depressed, indecisive, father conflict, mother conflict, lacks skills with the opposite sex, 8+ conferences.

246–X Anxieties, depressed, restless, indecisive, father conflict, lacks skills with the opposite sex, 8+ conferences.

247–0 Anxieties, depressed, insomnia, lacks self-confidence, indecisive, distractible in study, lacks academic drive, tense on examinations, lacks skills with the opposite sex, socially insecure (27), socially shy (27), socially extroverted (4–0), father conflict, rebellious toward home, 4 to 7 conferences. Note: Scale 0 coded low was infrequently associated with depression, lack of self-confidence, lack of skills with the opposite sex, social insecurity, social shyness; Scale 4 coded high was infrequently associated with social insecurity.

247–1 Anxieties, depressed, insomnia, lacks self-confidence, indecisive, physical inferiority, distractible in study, lacks skills with the opposite sex, socially insecure (27), socially shy (27), socially extroverted (4–1), father conflict, rebellious toward home, 4 to 7 conferences. Note: Scale 4 coded high was infrequently associated with social insecurity.

247–3 Anxieties, depressed, insomnia, lacks self-confidence, indecisive, distractible in study, lacks skills with the opposite sex, socially insecure, socially shy, father conflict, rebellious toward home, 4 to 7 conferences, cried in the interview. Note: Scale 4 coded high was infrequently associated with social insecurity.

247–5 Anxieties, depressed, nervous, headaches, exhaustion, insomnia, lacks self-confidence, indecisive, distractible in study, tense on examinations, lacks skills with the opposite sex, socially insecure, socially shy, father conflict, mother conflict, rebellious toward home, 4 to 7 conferences, wants answers. Note: Scale 4 coded high was infrequently associated with social insecurity.

247–6 Anxieties, depressed, insomnia, lacks self-confidence, indecisive, distractible in study, vague goals, lacks skills with the opposite sex, socially insecure, socially shy, father conflict, rebellious toward home, 4 to 7 conferences, nonverbal. Note: Scale 4 coded high was infrequently associated with social insecurity.

247–8 Anxieties, depressed, insomnia, lacks self-confidence, indecisive, distractible in study, lacks skills with the opposite sex, socially insecure,

FEMALE SECTION

socially shy, father conflict, rebellious toward home, 4 to 7 conferences. Note: Scale 4 coded high was infrequently associated with social insecurity.

247–9   Anxieties, depressed, insomnia, lacks self-confidence, indecisive, distractible in study, lacks skills with the opposite sex, socially insecure, socially shy, father conflict, rebellious toward home, mother conflict, 4 to 7 conferences. Note: Scale 4 coded high was infrequently associated with social insecurity.

247–X   Anxieties, depressed, insomnia, headaches, lacks self-confidence, indecisive, distractible in study, vague goals, lacks skills with the opposite sex, socially insecure, socially shy, father conflict, rebellious toward home, sibling conflict, 4 to 7 conferences. Note: Scale 4 coded high was infrequently associated with social insecurity.

248–0   Anxieties, depressed, insomnia, indecisive, distractible in study, lacks academic drive, tense on examinations, lacks skills with the opposite sex, socially extroverted, father conflict, overprotective mother, verbal. Note: Scale 0 coded low was infrequently associated with depression and lack of skills with the opposite sex.

248–1   Anxieties, depressed, insomnia, lacks self-confidence, indecisive, physical inferiority, distractible in study, lacks skills with the opposite sex, socially extroverted, father conflict, overprotective mother.

248–3   Anxieties, depressed, insomnia, indecisive, distractible in study, lacks skills with the opposite sex, father conflict, overprotective mother.

248–5   Anxieties, depressed, nervous, insomnia, indecisive, distractible in study, tense on examinations, lacks skills with the opposite sex, socially shy, socially insecure, father conflict, mother conflict, rebellious toward home, overprotective mother, wants answers.

248–6   Anxieties, depressed, insomnia, indecisive, lacks self-confidence, distractible in study, vague goals, lacks skills with the opposite sex, socially insecure, father conflict, overprotective mother, nonverbal.

248–7   Anxieties, depressed, insomnia, indecisive, distractible in study, lacks skills with the opposite sex, father conflict, overprotective mother.

248–9   Anxieties, depressed, insomnia, indecisive, distractible in study, lacks skills with the opposite sex, father conflict, mother conflict, overprotective mother.

248–X   Anxieties, depressed, headaches, insomnia, indecisive, distractible in study, lacks skills with the opposite sex, father conflict, mother conflict, sibling conflict, overprotective mother, 8+ conferences.

249–0   Anxieties, depressed, indecisive, lacks self-confidence, lacks skills with the opposite sex, socially insecure (29), socially extroverted (49, 4–0, 9–0, 49–0), father conflict, home conflict, tense on examinations, lacks academic drive, marriage oriented, vague goals, verbal. Note: Scale 0 coded low was infrequently associated with depression, lack of self-confidence, lack of skills with the opposite sex, social insecurity, home conflict.

249–1   Anxieties, depressed, indecisive, lacks self-confidence, physical inferiority, lacks skills with the opposite sex, socially insecure (29), socially extroverted (49, 4–1, 9–1, 49–1), father conflict, home conflict, vague goals, verbal.

249–3 Anxieties, depressed, indecisive, lacks self-confidence, lacks skills with the opposite sex, socially insecure (29), socially extroverted (49), father conflict, home conflict, vague goals, verbal.

249–5 Anxieties, depressed, nervous, exhaustion, indecisive, lacks self-confidence, lacks skills with the opposite sex, socially insecure (29, 2–5), socially shy (2–5), socially extroverted (49), father conflict, mother conflict, home conflict, rebellious toward home, vague goals, tense on examinations, verbal, wants answers.

249–6 Anxieties, depressed, indecisive, lacks self-confidence, lacks skills with the opposite sex, socially insecure (29, 2–6), socially extroverted (49), father conflict, home conflict, vague goals, verbal (49), nonverbal (2–6).

249–7/8 Anxieties, depressed, indecisive, lacks self-confidence, lacks skills with the opposite sex, socially insecure (29), socially extroverted (49), father conflict, home conflict, vague goals, verbal.

249–X Anxieties, depressed, indecisive, lacks self-confidence, lacks skills with the opposite sex, socially insecure (29), socially extroverted (49), father conflict, home conflict, vague goals, verbal.

25–0 Socially extroverted, tense on examinations.

25–1 Lacks self-confidence, physical inferiority.

25–4 Lacks self-confidence.

25–6 Lacks self-confidence, socially insecure, nonverbal.

25–9 Mother conflict.

25–X Depressed, distractible in study, lacks skills with the opposite sex. Note: Scale 5 coded high was infrequently associated with depression.

256–0 Anxieties, 8+ conferences, resistant in the interview, socially extroverted, tense on examinations. Note: Scale 5 coded high was infrequently associated with anxieties and 8+ conferences.

256–1 Anxieties, 8+ conferences, lacks self-confidence, physical inferiority. Note: Scale 5 coded high was infrequently associated with anxieties and 8+ conferences.

256–3 Anxieties, 8+ conferences. Note: Scale 5 coded high was infrequently associated with anxieties and 8+ conferences.

256–4 Anxieties, 8+ conferences, shy in the interview, lacks self-confidence. Note: Scale 5 coded high was infrequently associated with anxieties and 8+ conferences.

256–7/8 Anxieties, 8+ conferences. Note: Scale 5 coded high was infrequently associated with anxieties and 8+ conferences.

256–9 Anxieties, 8+ conferences, mother conflict. Note: Scale 5 coded high was infrequently associated with anxieties and 8+ conferences.

256–X Anxieties, restless, depressed, 8+ conferences, lacks skills with the opposite sex, distractible in study. Note: Scale 5 coded high was infrequently associated with anxieties and 8+ conferences.

257–0 Anxieties, depressed, lacks self-confidence, socially shy (27), socially insecure (27), socially extroverted (5–0), distractible in study, tense on examinations, 4 to 7 conferences. Note: Scale 5 coded high was infrequently associated with anxieties, depression, social shyness; Scale 0 coded low was infrequently associated with social shyness and social insecurity.

FEMALE SECTION

257–1 Anxieties, depressed, lacks self-confidence, physical inferiority, socially shy, socially insecure, distractible in study, 4 to 7 conferences. Note: Scale 5 coded high was infrequently associated with anxieties, depression, social shyness.

257–3 Anxieties, depressed, lacks self-confidence, socially shy, socially insecure, distractible in study, 4 to 7 conferences, cried in the interview. Note: Scale 5 coded high was infrequently associated with anxieties, depression, social shyness.

257–4 Anxieties, depressed, lacks self-confidence, socially shy, socially insecure, distractible in study, 4 to 7 conferences. Note: Scale 5 coded high was infrequently associated with anxieties, depression, social shyness.

257–6 Anxieties, depressed, lacks self-confidence, socially shy, socially insecure, distractible in study, 4 to 7 conferences, nonverbal. Note: Scale 5 coded high was infrequently associated with anxieties, depression, social shyness.

257–8 Anxieties, depressed, lacks self-confidence, socially shy, socially insecure, distractible in study, 4 to 7 conferences. Note: Scale 5 coded high was infrequently associated with anxieties, depression, social shyness.

257–9 Anxieties, depressed, lacks self-confidence, socially shy, socially insecure, distractible in study, 4 to 7 conferences, mother conflict. Note: Scale 5 coded high was infrequently associated with anxieties, depression, social shyness.

257–X Anxieties, depressed, headaches, lacks self-confidence, socially shy, socially insecure, lacks skills with the opposite sex, distractible in study, 4 to 7 conferences, sibling conflict. Note: Scale 5 coded high was infrequently associated with headaches, anxieties, depression, social shyness.

258–0 Anxieties, depressed, distractible in study, tense on examinations, lacks skills with the opposite sex, socially extroverted, verbal. Note: Scale 0 coded low was infrequently associated with depression and lack of skills with the opposite sex; Scale 5 coded high was infrequently associated with anxieties, depression, social shyness.

258–1 Anxieties, depressed, distractible in study, lacks skills with the opposite sex, lacks self-confidence, physical inferiority. Note: Scale 5 coded high was infrequently associated with anxieties, depression, social shyness.

258–3 Anxieties, depressed, distractible in study, lacks skills with the opposite sex. Note: Scale 5 coded high was infrequently associated with anxieties, depression, social shyness.

258–4 Anxieties, depressed, distractible in study, lacks skills with the opposite sex, lacks self-confidence. Note: Scale 5 coded high was infrequently associated with anxieties, depression, social shyness.

258–6 Anxieties, depressed, distractible in study, lacks skills with the opposite sex, socially insecure, lacks self-confidence, nonverbal. Note: Scale 5 coded high was infrequently associated with anxieties, depression, social shyness.

258–7 Anxieties, depressed, distractible in study, lacks skills with the opposite sex. Note: Scale 5 coded high was infrequently associated with anxieties, depression, social shyness.

258–9 Anxieties, depressed, distractible in study, lacks skills with the opposite sex, mother conflict. Note: Scale 5 coded high was infrequently associated with anxieties, depression, social shyness.

258–X   Anxieties, depressed, distractible in study, lacks skills with the opposite sex, 8+ conferences, father conflict, mother conflict, sibling conflict. Note: Scale 5 coded high was infrequently associated with father conflict, 8+ conferences, anxieties, depression.

259–0   Vague goals, tense on examinations, marriage oriented, lacks self-confidence, socially insecure (29), socially extroverted (59, 9–0, 5–0, 59–0), verbal. Note: Scale 0 coded low was infrequently associated with social insecurity and lack of self-confidence.

259–1   Vague goals, lacks self-confidence, physical inferiority, socially insecure (29), socially extroverted (59, 9–1).

259–3   Vague goals, lacks self-confidence, socially insecure (29), socially extroverted (59).

259–4   Vague goals, lacks self-confidence, socially insecure (29), socially extroverted (59), shy in the interview, nonresponsive.

259–6   Vague goals, lacks self-confidence, socially insecure (29), socially extroverted (59), nonverbal.

259–7/8   Vague goals, lacks self-confidence, socially insecure (29), socially extroverted (59).

259–X   Vague goals, distractible in study, lacks self-confidence, socially insecure (29), socially extroverted (59), lacks skills with the opposite sex, depressed. Note: Scale 5 coded high was infrequently associated with depression.

26–0   Anxieties, 8+ conferences, resistant in the interview, tense on examinations, socially extroverted.

26–1   Anxieties, 8+ conferences, lacks self-confidence, physical inferiority.

26–3   Anxieties, 8+ conferences.

26–4   Anxieties, 8+ conferences, shy in the interview, lacks self-confidence.

26–5   Anxieties, depressed, nervous, 8+ conferences, wants answers, nonresponsive, lacks skills with the opposite sex, socially shy, socially insecure, indecisive, physical inferiority.

26–7/8   Anxieties, 8+ conferences.

26–9   Anxieties, 8+ conferences, mother conflict.

26–X   Anxieties, depressed, restless, 8+ conferences, lacks skills with the opposite sex.

267–0   Anxieties, depressed, 8+ conferences (26), 4 to 7 conferences (27), resistant in the interview, lacks self-confidence, distractible in study, tense on examinations, socially shy (27), socially insecure (27), socially extroverted (6–0). Note: Scale 0 coded low was infrequently associated with depression, lack of self-confidence, social shyness, social insecurity.

267–1   Anxieties, depressed, 8+ conferences (26), 4 to 7 conferences (27), lacks self-confidence, physical inferiority, distractible in study, socially shy, socially insecure.

267–3   Anxieties, depressed, 8+ conferences (26), 4 to 7 conferences (27), cried in the interview, lacks self-confidence, distractible in study, socially shy, socially insecure.

267–4   Anxieties, depressed, 8+ conferences (26), 4 to 7 conferences (27), lacks self-confidence, distractible in study, socially shy, socially insecure, shy in the interview.

267–5   Anxieties, depressed, nervous, headaches, insomnia, exhaustion, 8+ conferences (26), 4 to 7 conferences (27), wants answers, nonresponsive, lacks self-confidence, indecisive, physical inferiority, distractible in study, tense on examinations, socially shy, socially insecure, lacks skills with the opposite sex.

267–8   Anxieties, depressed, 8+ conferences (26), 4 to 7 conferences (27), lacks self-confidence, distractible in study, socially shy, socially insecure.

267–9   Anxieties, depressed, headaches, restless, 8+ conferences (26), 4 to 7 conferences (27), lacks self-confidence, distractible in study, socially shy, socially insecure, lacks skills with the opposite sex, sibling conflict.

268–0   Anxieties, depressed, 8+ conferences, verbal, resistant in the interview, distractible in study, tense on examinations, lacks skills with the opposite sex, socially extroverted. Note: Scale 0 coded low was infrequently associated with depression and lack of skills with the opposite sex.

268–1   Anxieties, depressed, 8+ conferences, distractible in study, lacks skills with the opposite sex, lacks self-confidence, physical inferiority.

268–3   Anxieties, depressed, 8+ conferences, distractible in study, lacks skills with the opposite sex.

268–4   Anxieties, depressed, 8+ conferences, distractible in study, lacks skills with the opposite sex, shy in the interview, lacks self-confidence.

268–5   Anxieties, depressed, nervous, 8+ conferences, wants answers, nonresponsive, distractible in study, tense on examinations, lacks skills with the opposite sex, socially shy, socially insecure, physical inferiority, indecisive.

268–7   Anxieties, depressed, 8+ conferences, distractible in study, lacks skills with the opposite sex.

268–9   Anxieties, depressed, 8+ conferences, distractible in study, lacks skills with the opposite sex, mother conflict.

268–X   Anxieties, depressed, restless, 8+ conferences, distractible in study, lacks skills with the opposite sex, father conflict, mother conflict, sibling conflict.

269–0   Anxieties, lacks self-confidence, 8+ conferences, resistant in the interview, verbal, socially insecure (29), socially extroverted (6–0, 9–0), tense on examinations, marriage oriented. Note: Scale 0 coded low was infrequently associated with lack of self-confidence and social insecurity.

269–1   Anxieties, lacks self-confidence, physical inferiority, 8+ conferences, socially insecure (29), socially extroverted (9–1), vague goals.

269–3   Anxieties, lacks self-confidence, 8+ conferences, socially insecure, vague goals.

269–4   Anxieties, lacks self-confidence, 8+ conferences, nonresponsive, socially insecure, shy in the interview. Note: Scale 9 coded high was infrequently associated with shyness in the interview.

269–5   Anxieties, depressed, nervous, exhaustion, lacks self-confidence, indecisive, physical inferiority, 8+ conferences, wants answers, verbal, nonresponsive, socially insecure, socially shy, lacks skills with the opposite sex, tense on examinations.

269–7/8	Anxieties, lacks self-confidence, 8+ conferences, socially insecure.
269–X	Anxieties, restless, depressed, lacks self-confidence, 8+ conferences, socially insecure, lacks skills with the opposite sex.
27–0	Anxieties, depressed, lacks self-confidence, distractible in study, tense on examinations, socially shy, socially insecure, 4 to 7 conferences. Note: Scale 0 coded low was infrequently associated with depression, lack of self-confidence, social shyness, social insecurity.
27–1	Anxieties, depressed, lacks self-confidence, physical inferiority, distractible in study, socially shy, socially insecure, 4 to 7 conferences.
27–3	Anxieties, depressed, lacks self-confidence, distractible in study, socially shy, socially insecure, 4 to 7 conferences, cried in the interview.
27–4	Anxieties, depressed, lacks self-confidence, distractible in study, socially shy, socially insecure, 4 to 7 conferences.
27–5	Anxieties, depressed, nervous, headaches, insomnia, exhaustion, lacks self-confidence, indecisive, distractible in study, tense on examinations, socially shy, socially insecure, lacks skills with the opposite sex, 4 to 7 conferences, wants answers.
27–6	Anxieties, depressed, lacks self-confidence, distractible in study, socially shy, socially insecure, 4 to 7 conferences, nonverbal.
27–8	Anxieties, depressed, lacks self-confidence, distractible in study, socially shy, socially insecure, 4 to 7 conferences.
27–9	Anxieties, depressed, lacks self-confidence, distractible in study, socially shy, socially insecure, 4 to 7 conferences, mother conflict.
27–X	Anxieties, depressed, headaches, lacks self-confidence, distractible in study, socially shy, socially insecure, lacks skills with the opposite sex, 4 to 7 conferences, sibling conflict.
278–0	Anxieties, depressed, insomnia, nervous, lacks self-confidence, distractible in study, tense on examinations, socially insecure, socially shy, lacks skills with the opposite sex, 4 to 7 conferences, verbal. Note: Scale 0 coded low was infrequently associated with depression, lack of self-confidence, social insecurity, social shyness, lack of skills with the opposite sex.
278–1	Anxieties, depressed, insomnia, nervous, lacks self-confidence, physical inferiority, distractible in study, socially insecure, socially shy, lacks skills with the opposite sex, 4 to 7 conferences.
278–3	Anxieties, depressed, insomnia, nervous, lacks self-confidence, distractible in study, socially insecure, socially shy, lacks skills with the opposite sex, 4 to 7 conferences, cried in the interview.
278–4	Anxieties, depressed, insomnia, nervous, lacks self-confidence, distractible in study, socially insecure, socially shy, lacks skills with the opposite sex, 4 to 7 conferences.
278–5	Anxieties, depressed, insomnia, nervous, headaches, exhaustion, lacks self-confidence, indecisive, distractible in study, tense on examinations, socially insecure, socially shy, lacks skills with the opposite sex, 4 to 7 conferences, wants answers.
278–6	Anxieties, depressed, insomnia, nervous, lacks self-confidence, distractible in study, socially insecure, socially shy, lacks skills with the opposite sex, 4 to 7 conferences, nonverbal.

278–9 Anxieties, depressed, insomnia, nervous, lacks self-confidence distractible in study, socially insecure, socially shy, lacks skills with the opposite sex, 4 to 7 conferences, mother conflict.

278–X Anxieties, depressed, insomnia, nervous, exhaustion, headaches, lacks self-confidence, distractible in study, socially insecure, socially shy, lacks skills with the opposite sex, 4 to 7 conferences (27), 8+ conferences (28, 8–X), father conflict, mother conflict, sibling conflict.

279–0 Anxieties, depressed, nervous, exhaustion, lacks self-confidence, confused, distractible in study, tense on examinations, marriage oriented, socially insecure (29, 27), socially shy (27), socially extroverted (9–0), 4 to 7 conferences, verbal, sibling conflict. Note: Scale 0 coded low was infrequently associated with depression, exhaustion, lack of self-confidence, confusion, social shyness, social insecurity, sibling conflict.

279–1 Anxieties, depressed, nervous, lacks self-confidence, confused, physical inferiority, distractible in study, vague goals, socially insecure (29, 27), socially shy (27), socially extroverted (9–1), 4 to 7 conferences, sibling conflict.

279–3 Anxieties, depressed, nervous, lacks self-confidence, confused, distractible in study, vague goals, socially insecure, socially shy, 4 to 7 conferences, cried in the interview, sibling conflict.

279–4 Anxieties, depressed, nervous, lacks self-confidence, confused, distractible in study, socially insecure, socially shy, shy in the interview, 4 to 7 conferences, nonresponsive, sibling conflict. Note: Scale 9 coded high was infrequently associated with shyness in the interview.

279–5 Anxieties, depressed, nervous, headaches, insomnia, exhaustion, lacks self-confidence, confused, indecisive, distractible in study, tense on examinations, socially insecure, socially shy, lacks skills with the opposite sex, 4 to 7 conferences, wants answers, verbal, sibling conflict.

279–6 Anxieties, depressed, nervous, lacks self-confidence, confused, distractible in study, socially insecure, socially shy, 4 to 7 conferences, nonverbal, sibling conflict.

279–8 Anxieties, depressed, nervous, lacks self-confidence, confused, distractible in study, socially insecure, socially shy, 4 to 7 conferences, sibling conflict.

279–X Anxieties, depressed, nervous, headaches, lacks self-confidence, confused, distractible in study, socially insecure, socially shy, lacks skills with the opposite sex, 4 to 7 conferences, sibling conflict.

28–0 Anxieties, depressed, distractible in study, tense on examinations, verbal, lacks skills with the opposite sex. Note: Scale 0 coded low was infrequently associated with depression and lack of skills with the opposite sex.

28–1 Anxieties, depressed, distractible in study, lacks skills with the opposite sex, lacks self-confidence, physical inferiority.

28–3 Anxieties, depressed, distractible in study, lacks skills with the opposite sex.

28–4 Anxieties, depressed, distractible in study, lacks skills with the opposite sex, lacks self-confidence.

28–5 Anxieties, depressed, nervous, distractible in study, tense on examinations, lacks skills with the opposite sex, socially shy, socially insecure, indecisive, wants answers.

28–6   Anxieties, depressed, distractible in study, lacks skills with the opposite sex, socially insecure, lacks self-confidence, nonverbal.

28–7   Anxieties, depressed, distractible in study, lacks skills with the opposite sex.

28–9   Anxieties, depressed, distractible in study, lacks skills with the opposite sex, mother conflict.

28–X   Anxieties, depressed, distractible in study, lacks skills with the opposite sex, 8+ conferences, father conflict, mother conflict, sibling conflict.

289–0   Depressed, anxieties, restless, lacks self-confidence, confused, socially insecure (29), lacks skills with the opposite sex, socially extroverted (9–0), verbal, resistant in the interview, 8+ conferences, distractible in study, marriage oriented, tense on examinations. Note: Scale 0 coded low was infrequently associated with depression, lack of self-confidence, confusion, social insecurity, lack of skills with the opposite sex.

289–1   Depressed, anxieties, restless, lacks self-confidence, confused, physical inferiority, socially insecure (29), lacks skills with the opposite sex, socially extroverted (9–1), verbal, resistant in the interview, 8+ conferences, distractible in study.

289–3   Depressed, anxieties, restless, lacks self-confidence, confused, socially insecure, lacks skills with the opposite sex, verbal, resistant in the interview, 8+ conferences, distractible in study, vague goals.

289–4   Depressed, anxieties, restless, lacks self-confidence, confused, socially insecure, lacks skills with the opposite sex, shy in the interview, verbal, resistant in the interview, 8+ conferences, nonresponsive in the interview, distractible in study.

289–5   Depressed, anxieties, restless, nervous, exhaustion, lacks self-confidence, confused, indecisive, socially insecure, socially shy, lacks skills with the opposite sex, verbal, resistant in the interview, 8+ conferences, wants answers, distractible in study, tense on examinations. Note: Scale 5 coded low was infrequently associated with resistance in the interview.

289–6   Depressed, anxieties, restless, lacks self-confidence, confused, socially insecure, lacks skills with the opposite sex, verbal (89), resistant in the interview, 8+ conferences, nonverbal (2–6), distractible in study.

289–7   Depressed, anxieties, restless, lacks self-confidence, confused, socially insecure, lacks skills with the opposite sex, verbal, resistant in the interview, 8+ conferences, distractible in study.

289–X   Depressed, anxieties, restless, lacks self-confidence, confused, socially insecure, lacks skills with the opposite sex, verbal, resistant in the interview, 8+ conferences, distractible in study, father conflict, mother conflict, sibling conflict.

29–0   Lacks self-confidence, socially insecure (29), socially extroverted (9–0), verbal, marriage oriented, tense on examinations. Note: Scale 0 coded low was infrequently associated with lack of self-confidence and social insecurity.

29–1   Lacks self-confidence, physical inferiority, socially insecure (29), socially extroverted (9–1), vague goals.

29–3   Lacks self-confidence, socially insecure, vague goals.

FEMALE SECTION

29–4	Lacks self-confidence, socially insecure, shy in the interview, nonresponsive in the interview.
29–5	Lacks self-confidence, indecisive, socially insecure, socially shy, lacks skills with the opposite sex, verbal, wants answers, tense on examinations, depressed, nervous, anxieties, exhaustion.
29–6	Lacks self-confidence, socially insecure, nonverbal.
29–7/8	Lacks self-confidence, socially insecure.
29–X	Lacks self-confidence, socially insecure, lacks skills with the opposite sex, depressed.
3–0	Lacks academic drive, marriage oriented, tense on examinations, socially extroverted.
3–2	Socially extroverted.
3–5	Distractible in study, exhaustion, insomnia, headaches, home conflict.
3–X	Tense on examinations, verbal, father conflict, mother conflict.
34–0	Lacks academic drive, marriage oriented, tense on examinations, home conflict, socially extroverted. Note: Scale 0 coded low was infrequently associated with home conflict.
34–1	Lacks academic drive, home conflict, socially extroverted.
34–2	Lacks academic drive, home conflict, socially extroverted. Note: Scale 2 coded low was infrequently associated with home conflict.
34–5	Lacks academic drive, distractible in study, home conflict, rebellious toward home, lacks skills with the opposite sex, headaches, insomnia, exhaustion, anxieties, indecisive.
34–6	Lacks academic drive, vague goals, home conflict.
34–7/8/9	Lacks academic drive, home conflict.
34–X	Lacks academic drive, home conflict, father conflict, mother conflict, verbal, tense on examinations.
345–0	Home conflict, socially extroverted, marriage oriented, lacks academic drive, tense on examinations. Note: Scale 0 coded low was infrequently associated with home conflict.
345–1/2	Home conflict, socially extroverted, lacks academic drive.
345–6	Home conflict, vague goals, lacks academic drive.
345–7/8/9	Home conflict, lacks academic drive.
345–X	Home conflict, father conflict, mother conflict, verbal, lacks academic drive, tense on examinations, distractible in study.
346–0	Home conflict, resistant in the interview, tense on examinations, marriage oriented, lacks academic drive, socially extroverted. Note: Scale 0 coded low was infrequently associated with home conflict.
346–1	Home conflict, lacks academic drive, socially extroverted.
346–2	Home conflict, lacks academic drive, socially extroverted. Note: Scale 2 coded low was infrequently associated with home conflict.
346–5	Home conflict, rebellious toward home, lacks academic drive, distractible in study, anxieties, exhaustion, insomnia, headaches, lacks skills with the opposite sex, indecisive, physical inferiority.
346–7/8/9	Home conflict, lacks academic drive.
346–X	Home conflict, father conflict, mother conflict, lacks academic drive, tense on examinations, verbal, 8+ conferences, restless.

347–0   Anxieties, insomnia, home conflict, rebellious toward home, tense on examinations, marriage oriented, lacks academic drive, socially extroverted. Note: Scale 0 coded low was infrequently associated with home conflict.

347–1   Anxieties, insomnia, home conflict, rebellious toward home, lacks academic drive, socially extroverted.

347–2   Anxieties, insomnia, home conflict, rebellious toward home, lacks academic drive, socially extroverted. Note: Scale 2 coded low was infrequently associated with home conflict.

347–5   Anxieties, insomnia, headaches, exhaustion, nervous, home conflict, rebellious toward home, distractible in study, lacks academic drive, lacks skills with the opposite sex, socially insecure, lacks self-confidence, indecisive. Note: Scale 4 coded high was infrequently associated with social insecurity.

347–6   Anxieties, insomnia, home conflict, rebellious toward home, vague goals, lacks academic drive.

347–8/9   Anxieties, insomnia, home conflict, rebellious toward home, lacks academic drive.

347–X   Anxieties, insomnia, headaches, home conflict, rebellious toward home, father conflict, mother conflict, sibling conflict, tense on examinations, lacks academic drive, verbal.

348–0   Depressed, insomnia, home conflict, overprotective mother, tense on examinations, marriage oriented, lacks academic drive, socially extroverted, verbal. Note: Scale 0 coded low was infrequently associated with depression and home conflict.

348–1   Depressed, insomnia, home conflict, overprotective mother, lacks academic drive, socially extroverted, verbal.

348–2   Depressed (48), insomnia, home conflict, overprotective mother, lacks academic drive, socially extroverted, verbal. Note: Scale 2 coded low was infrequently associated with home conflict.

348–5   Depressed, insomnia, anxieties, headaches, exhaustion, home conflict, rebellious toward home, overprotective mother, distractible in study, lacks academic drive, lacks skills with the opposite sex, verbal, indecisive.

348–6   Depressed, insomnia, home conflict, overprotective mother, lacks academic drive, vague goals, verbal.

348–7/9   Depressed, insomnia, home conflict, overprotective mother, lacks academic drive, verbal.

348–X   Depressed, insomnia, headaches, home conflict, overprotective mother, mother conflict, father conflict, sibling conflict, tense on examinations, lacks academic drive, lacks skills with the opposite sex, verbal, 8+ conferences.

349–0   Home conflict, lacks academic drive, socially extroverted, verbal, marriage oriented, vague goals, tense on examinations.

349–1   Home conflict, lacks academic drive, marriage oriented, vague goals, socially extroverted, verbal.

349–2   Home conflict, lacks academic drive, marriage oriented, vague goals, socially extroverted, verbal. Note: Scale 2 coded low was infrequently associated with home conflict.

349–5	Home conflict, rebellious toward home, lacks academic drive, marriage oriented, vague goals, distractible in study, socially extroverted, lacks skills with the opposite sex, verbal, indecisive, anxieties, headaches, insomnia, exhaustion.
349–6/7/8	Home conflict, lacks academic drive, marriage oriented, vague goals, socially extroverted, verbal.
349–X	Home conflict, father conflict, mother conflict, lacks academic drive, marriage oriented, vague goals, tense on examinations, socially extroverted, verbal.
35–0	Lacks academic drive, marriage oriented, vague goals, socially extroverted.
35–2	Socially extroverted.
35–X	Distractible in study, tense on examinations, verbal, mother conflict, father conflict.
356–0	Lacks academic drive, marriage oriented, tense on examinations, socially extroverted, resistant in the interview.
356–2	Socially extroverted.
356–4	Shy in the interview.
356–X	Tense on examinations, distractible in study, restless, verbal, 8+ conferences, father conflict, mother conflict. Note: Scale 5 coded high was infrequently associated with 8+ conferences, father conflict.
357–0	Anxieties, insomnia, lacks academic drive, marriage oriented, tense on examinations, socially extroverted. Note: Scale 5 coded high was infrequently associated with anxieties.
357–1	Anxieties, insomnia. Note: Scale 5 coded high was infrequently associated with anxieties.
357–2	Anxieties, insomnia, socially extroverted. Note: Scale 5 coded high was infrequently associated with anxieties.
357–4/6/8/9	Anxieties, insomnia. Note: Scale 5 coded high was infrequently associated with anxieties.
357–X	Anxieties, insomnia, headaches, tense on examinations, distractible in study, verbal, father conflict, mother conflict, sibling conflict. Note: Scale 5 coded high was infrequently associated with headaches, father conflict, anxieties.
358–0	Tense on examinations, marriage oriented, lacks academic drive, verbal, socially extroverted.
358–1	Verbal.
358–2	Verbal, socially extroverted.
358–4/6/7/9	Verbal.
358–X	Verbal, 8+ conferences, depressed, tense on examinations, distractible in study, lacks skills with the opposite sex, mother conflict, father conflict, sibling conflict. Note: Scale 5 coded high was infrequently associated with depression and father conflict.
359–0	Socially extroverted, marriage oriented, lacks academic drive, tense on examinations, vague goals, verbal.
359–1/2	Socially extroverted, marriage oriented, vague goals.
359–4	Socially extroverted, shy in the interview, marriage oriented, vague goals, nonresponsive.

359–6/7/8	Socially extroverted, marriage oriented, vague goals.
359–X	Socially extroverted, marriage oriented, vague goals, tense on examinations, distractible in study, verbal, father conflict, mother conflict. Note: Scale 5 coded high was infrequently associated with father conflict.
36–0	Lacks academic drive, marriage oriented, tense on examinations, socially extroverted, resistant in the interview.
36–2	Socially extroverted.
36–4	Shy in the interview.
36–5	Exhaustion, insomnia, headaches, distractible in study, physical inferiority, home conflict.
36–X	Verbal, 8+ conferences, tense on examinations, restless, father conflict, mother conflict.
367–0	Anxieties, insomnia, lacks academic drive, marriage oriented, tense on examinations, socially extroverted, resistant in the interview.
367–1	Anxieties, insomnia.
367–2	Anxieties, insomnia, socially extroverted.
367–4	Anxieties, insomnia, shy in the interview.
367–5	Anxieties, insomnia, headaches, exhaustion, nervous, distractible in study, socially insecure, physical inferiority, lacks self-confidence, indecisive, home conflict. Note: Scale 3 coded high was infrequently associated with social insecurity.
367–8/9	Anxieties, insomnia.
367–X	Anxieties, insomnia, restless, headaches, tense on examinations, verbal, 8+ conferences, father conflict, mother conflict, sibling conflict.
368–0	Tense on examinations, marriage oriented, lacks academic drive, socially extroverted, verbal, 8+ conferences, resistant in the interview.
368–1	Verbal, 8+ conferences.
368–2	Verbal, 8+ conferences, socially extroverted.
368–4	Verbal, 8+ conferences, shy in the interview.
368–5	Verbal, 8+ conferences, exhaustion, headaches, insomnia, anxieties, distractible in study, physical inferiority, home conflict.
368–7/9	Verbal, 8+ conferences.
368–X	Verbal, 8+ conferences, depressed, restless, tense on examinations, lacks skills with the opposite sex, father conflict, mother conflict, sibling conflict.
369–0	Marriage oriented, lacks academic drive, tense on examinations, socially extroverted, verbal, resistant in the interview.
369–1	Marriage oriented, vague goals, socially extroverted.
369–2	Marriage oriented, socially extroverted.
369–4	Marriage oriented, socially extroverted, shy in the interview, nonresponsive. Note: Scale 3 coded high was infrequently associated with nonresponsiveness.
369–5	Marriage oriented, distractible in study, socially extroverted, headaches, insomnia, exhaustion, physical inferiority, verbal, home conflict.
369–7/8	Marriage oriented, socially extroverted.
369–X	Marriage oriented, tense on examinations, socially extroverted, restless, verbal, 8+ conferences, father conflict, mother conflict.
37–0	Anxieties, insomnia, lacks academic drive, marriage oriented, tense on examinations, socially extroverted.

FEMALE SECTION

37–1	Anxieties, insomnia.
37–2	Anxieties, insomnia, socially extroverted.
37–4	Anxieties, insomnia.
37–5	Anxieties, insomnia, headaches, exhaustion, nervous, distractible in study, home conflict, lacks self-confidence, indecisive, shy in the interview. Note: Scale 3 coded high was infrequently associated with shyness in the interview.
37–6/8/9	Anxieties, insomnia.
37–X	Anxieties, insomnia, headaches, nervous, lacks self-confidence, tense on examinations, verbal, father conflict, mother conflict, sibling conflict.
378–0	Anxieties, insomnia, nervous, lacks self-confidence, verbal, marriage oriented, lacks academic drive, tense on examinations, socially extroverted. Note: Scale 0 coded low was infrequently associated with lack of self-confidence.
378–1	Anxieties, insomnia, nervous, lacks self-confidence, verbal.
378–2	Anxieties, insomnia, nervous, lacks self-confidence, verbal, socially extroverted. Note: Scale 2 coded low was infrequently associated with lack of self-confidence.
378–4	Anxieties, insomnia, nervous, lacks self-confidence, verbal.
378–5	Anxieties, insomnia, nervous, headaches, exhaustion, lacks self-confidence, indecisive, verbal, distractible in study, socially insecure, home conflict. Note: Scale 3 coded high was infrequently associated with social insecurity.
378–6/9	Anxieties, insomnia, nervous, lacks self-confidence, verbal.
378–X	Anxieties, insomnia, depressed, headaches, exhaustion, nervous, lacks self-confidence, verbal, 8+ conferences, tense on examinations, lacks skills with the opposite sex, father conflict, mother conflict, sibling conflict.
379–0	Anxieties, insomnia, nervous, exhaustion, marriage oriented, distractible in study, tense on examinations, lacks academic drive, socially extroverted, verbal, confused, sibling conflict. Note: Scale 0 coded low was infrequently associated with exhaustion, confusion, sibling conflict.
379–1	Anxieties, insomnia, nervous, marriage oriented, distractible in study, vague goals, socially extroverted, confused, sibling conflict. Note: Scale 1 coded low was infrequently associated with sibling conflict.
379–2	Anxieties, insomnia, nervous, marriage oriented, distractible in study, socially extroverted, confused, sibling conflict. Note: Scale 2 coded low was infrequently associated with confusion.
379–4	Anxieties, insomnia, nervous, marriage oriented, distractible in study, socially extroverted, shy in the interview, nonresponsive, confused, sibling conflict.
379–5	Anxieties, insomnia, nervous, headaches, exhaustion, marriage oriented, distractible in study, socially extroverted (39), socially insecure (7–5), verbal, confused, lacks self-confidence, indecisive, sibling conflict, home conflict.
379–6/8	Anxieties, insomnia, nervous, marriage oriented, distractible in study, socially extroverted, confused, sibling conflict.
379–X	Anxieties, insomnia, nervous, headaches, marriage oriented, distractible

111

in study, tense on examinations, socially extroverted, verbal, confused, sibling conflict, father conflict, mother conflict.

38–0	Verbal, lacks academic drive, marriage oriented, tense on examinations, socially extroverted.
38–1	Verbal.
38–2	Verbal, socially extroverted.
38–4	Verbal.
38–5	Verbal, insomnia, headaches, exhaustion, anxieties, home conflict, distractible in study.
38–6/7/9	Verbal.
38–X	Verbal, depressed, lacks skills with the opposite sex, 8+ conferences, tense on examinations, sibling conflict, father conflict, mother conflict.
389–0	Verbal, 8+ conferences, resistant in the interview, marriage oriented, tense on examinations, lacks academic drive, socially extroverted, confused, restless. Note: Scale 0 coded low was infrequently associated with confusion.
389–1	Verbal, resistant in the interview, 8+ conferences, marriage oriented, vague goals, socially extroverted, confused, restless.
389–2	Verbal, 8+ conferences, resistant in the interview, marriage oriented, socially extroverted, confused, restless, exhaustion. Note: Scale 2 coded low was infrequently associated with confusion.
389–4	Verbal, 8+ conferences, resistant in the interview, nonresponsive, marriage oriented, socially extroverted, shy in the interview, confused, restless.
389–5	Verbal, 8+ conferences, resistant in the interview, wants answers, marriage oriented, distractible in study, socially extroverted, confused, restless, headaches, insomnia, exhaustion, anxieties, family conflict. Note: Scale 5 coded low was infrequently associated with resistance in the interview.
389–6/7	Verbal, 8+ conferences, resistant in the interview, marriage oriented, socially extroverted, confused, restless.
389–X	Verbal, 8+ conferences, resistant in the interview, marriage oriented, tense on examinations, socially extroverted, lacks skills with the opposite sex, confused, restless, depressed, father conflict, mother conflict, sibling conflict.
39–0	Marriage oriented, tense on examinations, lacks academic drive, socially extroverted, verbal.
39–1	Marriage oriented, vague goals, socially extroverted.
39–2	Marriage oriented, socially extroverted.
39–4	Marriage oriented, socially extroverted, shy in the interview, nonresponsive. Note: Scale 9 coded high was infrequently associated with shyness in the interview.
39–5	Marriage oriented, distractible in study, socially extroverted, verbal, headaches, insomnia, exhaustion, home conflict.
39–6/7/8	Marriage oriented, socially extroverted.
39–X	Marriage oriented, tense on examinations, socially extroverted, verbal, mother conflict, father conflict.

FEMALE SECTION

4–0	Lacks academic drive, socially extroverted.
4–1/2	Socially extroverted.
4–5	Lacks skills with the opposite sex, indecisive, rebellious toward home, anxieties.
4–6	Vague goals.
45–0	Socially extroverted, lacks academic drive.
45–1/2	Socially extroverted.
45–6	Vague goals.
45–X	Distractible in study.
456–0	Socially extroverted, lacks academic drive, resistant in the interview.
456–1/2	Socially extroverted.
456–X	Restless, 8+ conferences, distractible in study. Note: Scale 5 coded high was infrequently associated with 8+ conferences.
457–0	Insomnia, rebellious toward home, socially extroverted, lacks academic drive.
457–1/2	Insomnia, rebellious toward home, socially extroverted.
457–3	Insomnia, rebellious toward home, cried in the interview.
457–6	Insomnia, rebellious toward home, vague goals.
457–8/9	Insomnia, rebellious toward home.
457–X	Insomnia, headaches, rebellious toward home, sibling conflict, distractible in study, tense on examinations.
458–0	Depressed, insomnia, overprotective mother, socially extroverted, lacks academic drive, verbal. Note: Scale 5 coded high and Scale 0 coded low were infrequently associated with depression.
458–1	Depressed, insomnia, overprotective mother, socially extroverted. Note: Scale 5 coded high was infrequently associated with depression.
458–2	Depressed (48), insomnia, overprotective mother, socially extroverted. Note: Scale 5 coded high was infrequently associated with depression.
458–3/6/7/9	Depressed, insomnia, overprotective mother. Note: Scale 5 coded high was infrequently associated with depression.
458–X	Depressed, insomnia, headaches, overprotective mother, mother conflict, father conflict, sibling conflict, distractible in study, lacks skills with the opposite sex, 8+ conferences. Note: Scale 5 coded high was infrequently associated with depression and father conflict.
459–0	Vague goals, marriage oriented, lacks academic drive, verbal, home conflict, socially extroverted. Note: Scale 0 coded low was infrequently associated with home conflict.
459–1	Vague goals, verbal, home conflict, socially extroverted.
459–2	Vague goals, verbal, home conflict, socially extroverted. Note: Scale 2 coded low was infrequently associated with home conflict.
459–3/6/7/8	Vague goals, verbal, home conflict, socially extroverted.
459–X	Vague goals, distractible in study, verbal, home conflict, socially extroverted.
46–0	Lacks academic drive, socially extroverted, resistant in the interview.

46–1/2	Socially extroverted.
46–5	Rebellious toward home, physical inferiority, indecisive, anxieties, lacks skills with the opposite sex.
46–X	Restless, 8+ conferences.
467–0	Insomnia, rebellious toward home, socially extroverted, lacks academic drive, resistant in the interview.
467–1/2	Insomnia, rebellious toward home, socially extroverted.
467–3	Insomnia, rebellious toward home, cried in the interview.
467–5	Insomnia, anxieties, headaches, exhaustion, nervous, rebellious toward home, lacks skills with the opposite sex, socially insecure, indecisive, physical inferiority, lacks self-confidence. Note: Scale 3 coded high was infrequently associated with social insecurity.
467–8/9	Insomnia, rebellious toward home.
467–X	Insomnia, restless, headaches, rebellious toward home, sibling conflict, tense on examinations, 8+ conferences.
468–0	Depressed, insomnia, overprotective mother, socially extroverted, lacks academic drive, resistant in the interview, verbal, 8+ conferences.
468–1/2	Depressed (48), insomnia, overprotective mother, socially extroverted, 8+ conferences.
468–3	Depressed, insomnia, overprotective mother, 8+ conferences.
468–5	Depressed, insomnia, anxieties, overprotective mother, rebellious toward home, lacks skills with the opposite sex, distractible in study, physical inferiority, indecisive, 8+ conferences.
468–7/9	Depressed, insomnia, overprotective mother, 8+ conferences.
468–X	Depressed, insomnia, headaches, restless, overprotective mother, mother conflict, father conflict, sibling conflict, lacks skills with the opposite sex, 8+ conferences.
469–0	Vague goals, lacks academic drive, marriage oriented, verbal, resistant in the interview, home conflict, socially extroverted. Note: Scale 0 coded low was infrequently associated with home conflict.
469–1	Vague goals, verbal, home conflict, socially extroverted.
469–2	Vague goals, verbal, home conflict, socially extroverted. Note: Scale 2 coded low was infrequently associated with home conflict.
469–3	Vague goals, verbal, home conflict, socially extroverted.
469–5	Vague goals, verbal, home conflict, rebellious toward home, socially extroverted, lacks skills with the opposite sex, indecisive, physical inferiority, anxieties, exhaustion.
469–7/8	Vague goals, verbal, home conflict, socially extroverted.
469–X	Vague goals, verbal, 8+ conferences, home conflict, socially extroverted, restless.
47–0	Insomnia, rebellious toward home, lacks academic drive, socially extroverted.
47–1/2	Insomnia, rebellious toward home, socially extroverted.
47–3	Insomnia, rebellious toward home, cried in the interview.
47–5	Insomnia, anxieties, headaches, exhaustion, nervous, rebellious toward home, indecisive, lacks self-confidence, socially insecure, lacks skills with the opposite sex.
47–6	Insomnia, rebellious toward home, vague goals.
47–8/9	Insomnia, rebellious toward home.

FEMALE SECTION

47–X   Insomnia, headaches, rebellious toward home, sibling conflict, tense on examinations.

478–0   Insomnia, depressed, nervous, rebellious toward home, overprotective mother, socially extroverted, lacks academic drive, verbal, lacks self-confidence. Note: Scale 0 coded low was infrequently associated with depression and lack of self-confidence.

478–1   Insomnia, depressed, nervous, rebellious toward home, overprotective mother, socially extroverted, lacks self-confidence.

478–2   Insomnia, depressed (48), nervous, rebellious toward home, overprotective mother, socially extroverted, lacks self-confidence. Note: Scale 2 coded low was infrequently associated with lack of self-confidence.

478–3   Insomnia, depressed, nervous, rebellious toward home, overprotective mother, lacks self-confidence, cried in the interview.

478–5   Insomnia, depressed, nervous, anxieties, headaches, exhaustion, rebellious toward home, overprotective mother, lacks skills with the opposite sex, socially insecure, distractible in study, lacks self-confidence, indecisive. Note: Scale 4 coded high was infrequently associated with social insecurity.

478–6   Insomnia, depressed, nervous, rebellious toward home, overprotective mother, vague goals, lacks self-confidence.

478–9   Insomnia, depressed, nervous, rebellious toward home, overprotective mother, lacks self-confidence.

478–X   Insomnia, depressed, nervous, exhaustion, headaches, rebellious toward home, overprotective mother, mother conflict, father conflict, sibling conflict, lacks skills with the opposite sex, tense on examinations, lacks self-confidence, 8+ conferences.

479–0   Insomnia, nervous, exhaustion, rebellious toward home, sibling conflict, home conflict, confused, distractible in study, vague goals, marriage oriented, lacks academic drive, verbal, socially extroverted. Note: Scale 0 coded low was infrequently associated with exhaustion, sibling conflict, home conflict, confusion.

479–1   Insomnia, nervous, rebellious toward home, sibling conflict, home conflict, confused, distractible in study, vague goals, verbal, socially extroverted.

479–2   Insomnia, nervous, rebellious toward home, sibling conflict, home conflict, confused, distractible in study, vague goals, verbal, socially extroverted. Note: Scale 2 coded low was infrequently associated with home conflict and confusion.

479–3   Insomnia, nervous, rebellious toward home, sibling conflict, home conflict, confused, distractible in study, vague goals, verbal, cried in the interview, socially extroverted.

479–5   Insomnia, nervous, anxieties, exhaustion, headaches, rebellious toward home, sibling conflict, home conflict, confused, indecisive, lacks self-confidence, distractible in study, vague goals, verbal, socially extroverted (49), lacks skills with the opposite sex, socially insecure (7–5).

479–6/8   Insomnia, nervous, rebellious toward home, sibling conflict, home conflict, confused, distractible in study, vague goals, verbal, socially extroverted.

479–X	Insomnia, nervous, headaches, rebellious toward home, sibling conflict, home conflict, confused, distractible in study, vague goals, tense on examinations, verbal, socially extroverted.
48–0	Depressed, insomnia, overprotective mother, socially extroverted, lacks academic drive, verbal. Note: Scale 0 coded low was infrequently associated with depression.
48–1	Depressed, insomnia, overprotective mother, socially extroverted.
48–2	Depressed (48), insomnia, overprotective mother, socially extroverted.
48–3	Depressed, insomnia, overprotective mother.
48–5	Depressed, insomnia, anxieties, overprotective mother, rebellious toward home, lacks skills with the opposite sex, indecisive, distractible in study.
48–6	Depressed, insomnia, overprotective mother, vague goals.
48–7/9	Depressed, insomnia, overprotective mother.
48–X	Depressed, insomnia, headaches, overprotective mother, mother conflict, father conflict, sibling conflict, lacks skills with the opposite sex, 8+ conferences.
489–0	Depressed, insomnia, restless, confused, overprotective mother, home conflict, socially extroverted, vague goals, lacks academic drive, marriage oriented, verbal, 8+ conferences, resistant in the interview. Note: Scale 0 coded low was infrequently associated with depression, confusion, home conflict.
489–1	Depressed, insomnia, restless, confused, overprotective mother, home conflict, socially extroverted, vague goals, verbal, 8+ conferences, resistant in the interview.
489–2	Depressed (48), insomnia, exhaustion, restless, confused, overprotective mother, home conflict, socially extroverted, vague goals, verbal, 8+ conferences, resistant in the interview. Note: Scale 2 coded low was infrequently associated with confusion and home conflict.
489–3	Depressed, insomnia, restless, confused, overprotective mother, home conflict, socially extroverted, vague goals, verbal, 8+ conferences, resistant in the interview.
489–5	Depressed, insomnia, restless, exhaustion, anxieties, confused, indecisive, overprotective mother, home conflict, rebellious toward home, socially extroverted, lacks skills with the opposite sex, vague goals, distractible in study, verbal, 8+ conferences, resistant in the interview, wants answers. Note: Scale 5 coded low was infrequently associated with resistance in the interview.
489–6/7	Depressed, insomnia, restless, confused, overprotective mother, home conflict, socially extroverted, vague goals, verbal, 8+ conferences, resistant in the interview.
489–X	Depressed, insomnia, headaches, restless, confused, overprotective mother, home conflict, mother conflict, father conflict, sibling conflict, socially extroverted, lacks skills with the opposite sex, vague goals, verbal, 8+ conferences, resistant in the interview.
49–0	Vague goals, lacks academic drive, marriage oriented, verbal, home conflict, socially extroverted. Note: Scale 0 coded low was infrequently associated with home conflict.
49–1	Vague goals, verbal, home conflict, socially extroverted.

FEMALE SECTION

49–2 Vague goals, verbal, home conflict, socially extroverted. Note: Scale 2 coded low was infrequently associated with home conflict.

49–3 Vague goals, verbal, home conflict, socially extroverted.

49–5 Vague goals, verbal, home conflict, rebellious toward home, socially extroverted, lacks skills with the opposite sex, indecisive, anxieties, exhaustion.

49–6/7/8/X Vague goals, verbal, home conflict, socially extroverted.

5–0 Socially extroverted.

5–X Distractible in study.

56–0 Socially extroverted, resistant in the interview.

56–2 Socially extroverted.

56–4 Shy in the interview.

56–X Restless, 8+ conferences, distractible in study. Note: Scale 5 coded high was infrequently associated with 8+ conferences.

567–0 Socially extroverted, resistant in the interview.

567–2 Socially extroverted.

567–3 Cried in the interview.

567–4 Shy in the interview.

567–X Restless, headaches, 8+ conferences, distractible in study, sibling conflict. Note: Scale 5 coded high was infrequently associated with headaches and 8+ conferences.

568–0 8+ conferences, resistant in the interview, verbal, socially extroverted. Note: Scale 5 coded high was infrequently associated with 8+ conferences.

568–1 8+ conferences. Note: Scale 5 coded high was infrequently associated with 8+ conferences.

568–2 8+ conferences, socially extroverted. Note: Scale 5 coded high was infrequently associated with 8+ conferences.

568–3 8+ conferences. Note: Scale 5 coded high was infrequently associated with 8+ conferences.

568–4 8+ conferences, shy in the interview. Note: Scale 5 coded high was infrequently associated with 8+ conferences.

568–7/9 8+ conferences. Note: Scale 5 coded high was infrequently associated with 8+ conferences.

568–X 8+ conferences, restless, depressed, distractible in study, lacks skills with the opposite sex, mother conflict, father conflict, sibling conflict. Note: Scale 5 coded high was infrequently associated with 8+ conferences, depression, father conflict.

569–0 Socially extroverted, vague goals, marriage oriented, resistant in the interview, verbal.

569–1/2/3 Socially extroverted, vague goals.

569–4 Socially extroverted, shy in the interview, vague goals, nonresponsive.

569–7/8 Socially extroverted, vague goals.

569–X Socially extroverted, vague goals, distractible in study, restless, 8+ conferences. Note: Scale 5 coded high was infrequently associated with 8+ conferences.

57–0 Socially extroverted.

57–3 Cried in the interview.

CODEBOOK OF MMPI PATTERNS

57–X	Headaches, sibling conflict, distractible in study. Note: Scale 5 coded high was infrequently associated with headaches.
578–0	Insomnia, nervous, lacks self-confidence, socially extroverted, verbal.
578–1	Insomnia, nervous, lacks self-confidence.
578–2	Insomnia, nervous, lacks self-confidence. Note: Scale 2 coded low was infrequently associated with lack of self-confidence.
578–3	Insomnia, nervous, lacks self-confidence, cried in the interview.
578–4/6/9	Insomnia, nervous, lacks self-confidence.
578–X	Insomnia, headaches, nervous, exhaustion, depressed, 8+ conferences, lacks self-confidence, distractible in study, mother conflict, father conflict, sibling conflict, lacks skills with the opposite sex. Note: Scale 5 coded high was infrequently associated with 8+ conferences, depression, father conflict.
579–0	Vague goals, distractible in study, marriage oriented, socially extroverted, sibling conflict, confused, nervous, exhaustion, verbal. Note: Scale 0 coded low was infrequently associated with sibling conflict, confusion, exhaustion.
579–1	Vague goals, distractible in study, socially extroverted, sibling conflict, confused, nervous. Note: Scale 1 coded low was infrequently associated with sibling conflict.
579–2	Vague goals, distractible in study, socially extroverted, sibling conflict, confused, nervous. Note: Scale 2 coded low was infrequently associated with confusion.
579–3	Vague goals, distractible in study, socially extroverted, sibling conflict, confused, nervous, cried in the interview.
579–4	Vague goals, distractible in study, socially extroverted, shy in the interview, sibling conflict, confused, nervous, nonresponsive.
579–6/8	Vague goals, distractible in study, socially extroverted, sibling conflict, confused, nervous.
579–X	Vague goals, distractible in study, socially extroverted, sibling conflict, confused, nervous, headaches.
58–0	Socially extroverted, verbal.
58–X	Lacks skills with the opposite sex, 8+ conferences, distractible in study, sibling conflict, father conflict, mother conflict, depression. Note: Scale 5 coded high was infrequently associated with 8+ conferences, father conflict, depression.
589–0	Vague goals, marriage oriented, socially extroverted, restless, confused, 8+ conferences, verbal, resistant in the interview. Note: Scale 0 coded low was infrequently associated with confusion; Scale 5 coded high was infrequently associated with 8+ conferences.
589–1	Vague goals, socially extroverted, restless, exhaustion, confused, 8+ conferences, verbal, resistant in the interview. Note: Scale 5 coded high was infrequently associated with 8+ conferences.
589–2	Vague goals, socially extroverted, restless, exhaustion, confused, 8+ conferences, verbal, resistant in the interview. Note: Scale 2 coded low was infrequently associated with confusion; Scale 5 coded high was infrequently associated with 8+ conferences.
589–3	Vague goals, socially extroverted, restless, confused, 8+ conferences,

	verbal, resistant in the interview. Note: Scale 5 coded high was infrequently associated with 8+ conferences.
589–4	Vague goals, socially extroverted, shy in the interview, restless, confused, 8+ conferences, verbal, resistant in the interview, nonresponsive. Note: Scale 5 coded high was infrequently associated with 8+ conferences.
589–6/7	Vague goals, socially extroverted, restless, confused, 8+ conferences, verbal, resistant in the interview. Note: Scale 5 coded high was infrequently associated with 8+ conferences.
589–X	Vague goals, distractible in study, socially extroverted, lacks skills with the opposite sex, restless, confused, depressed, 8+ conferences, verbal, resistant in the interview, father conflict, mother conflict, sibling conflict. Note: Scale 5 coded high was infrequently associated with depression, 8+ conferences, father conflict.
59–0	Vague goals, marriage oriented, socially extroverted, verbal.
59–1/2/3	Vague goals, socially extroverted.
59–4	Vague goals, socially extroverted, shy in the interview, nonresponsive. Note: Scale 9 coded high was infrequently associated with shyness in the interview.
59–6/7/8	Vague goals, socially extroverted.
59–X	Vague goals, distractible in study, socially extroverted.
6–0	Socially extroverted, resistant in the interview.
6–2	Socially extroverted.
6–4	Shy in the interview.
6–5	Physical inferiority.
67–0	Socially extroverted, resistant in the interview.
67–2	Socially extroverted.
67–3	Cried in the interview.
67–4	Shy in the interview.
67–5	Physical inferiority, indecisive, lacks self-confidence, exhaustion, nervous, anxieties, headaches, insomnia, socially insecure.
67–X	Restless, headaches, 8+ conferences, sibling conflict.
678–0	Insomnia, nervous, lacks self-confidence, 8+ conferences, resistant in the interview, verbal, socially extroverted. Note: Scale 0 coded low was infrequently associated with lack of self-confidence.
678–1	Insomnia, nervous, lacks self-confidence, 8+ conferences.
678–2	Insomnia, nervous, lacks self-confidence, 8+ conferences, socially extroverted. Note: Scale 2 coded low was infrequently associated with lack of self-confidence.
678–3	Insomnia, nervous, lacks self-confidence, 8+ conferences, cried in the interview.
678–4	Insomnia, nervous, lacks self-confidence, 8+ conferences, shy in the interview.
678–5	Insomnia, nervous, headaches, exhaustion, anxieties, lacks self-confidence, physical inferiority, indecisive, 8+ conferences, socially insecure, distractible in study.
678–9	Insomnia, nervous, lacks self-confidence, 8+ conferences.
678–X	Insomnia, nervous, restless, headaches, depressed, exhaustion, lacks

self-confidence, 8+ conferences, father conflict, mother conflict, sibling conflict, lacks skills with the opposite sex.

679–0   Nervous, exhaustion, confused, distractible in study, marriage oriented, sibling conflict, resistant in the interview, verbal, socially extroverted. Note: Scale 0 coded low was infrequently associated with exhaustion, confusion, sibling conflict.

679–1   Nervous, confused, distractible in study, vague goals, sibling conflict, socially extroverted. Note: Scale 1 coded low was infrequently associated with sibling conflict.

679–2   Nervous, confused, distractible in study, sibling conflict, socially extroverted. Note: Scale 2 coded low was infrequently associated with confusion.

679–3   Nervous, confused, distractible in study, vague goals, sibling conflict, cried in the interview.

679–4   Nervous, confused, distractible in study, sibling conflict, nonresponsive, shy in the interview. Note: Scale 9 coded high was infrequently associated with shyness in the interview.

679–5   Nervous, headaches, insomnia, exhaustion, anxieties, confused, distractible in study, sibling conflict, verbal, socially insecure, lacks self-confidence, physical inferiority, indecisive.

679–8   Nervous, confused, distractible in study, sibling conflict.

679–X   Nervous, restless, headaches, confused, distractible in study, sibling conflict, 8+ conferences.

68–0   Socially extroverted, 8+ conferences, verbal, resistant in the interview.

68–1   8+ conferences.

68–2   8+ conferences, socially extroverted.

68–3   8+ conferences.

68–4   8+ conferences, shy in the interview.

68–5   8+ conferences, physical inferiority, distractible in study, anxieties.

68–7/9   8+ conferences.

68–X   8+ conferences, restless, depressed, lacks skills with the opposite sex, father conflict, mother conflict, sibling conflict.

689–0   Restless, resistant in the interview, verbal, 8+ conferences, confused, socially extroverted, marriage oriented. Note: Scale 0 coded low was infrequently associated with confusion.

689–1   Restless, resistant in the interview, verbal, 8+ conferences, confused, socially extroverted, vague goals.

689–2   Restless, exhaustion, resistant in the interview, verbal, 8+ conferences, confused, socially extroverted. Note: Scale 2 coded low was infrequently associated with confusion.

689–3   Restless, resistant in the interview, verbal, 8+ conferences, confused.

689–4   Restless, resistant in the interview, verbal, 8+ conferences, nonresponsive, confused, shy in the interview. Note: Scale 9 coded high was infrequently associated with shyness in the interview.

689–5   Restless, anxieties, exhaustion, resistant in the interview, verbal, 8+ conferences, cried in the interview, confused, physical inferiority, distractible in study. Note: Scale 5 coded low was infrequently associated with resistance in the interview.

FEMALE SECTION

689–7	Restless, resistant in the interview, verbal, 8+ conferences, confused.
689–X	Restless, depressed, resistant in the interview, verbal, 8+ conferences, confused, lacks skills with the opposite sex, father conflict, mother conflict, sibling conflict.
69–0	Resistant in the interview, verbal, marriage oriented, socially extroverted.
69–1	Vague goals, socially extroverted.
69–2	Socially extroverted.
69–3	Vague goals.
69–4	Shy in the interview, nonresponsive. Note: Scale 9 coded high was infrequently associated with shyness in the interview.
69–5	Exhaustion, verbal, physical inferiority.
69–X	Restless, 8+ conferences.
7–3	Cried in the interview.
7–5	Anxieties, nervous, exhaustion, insomnia, headaches, lacks self-confidence, indecisive, socially insecure.
7–X	Headaches, sibling conflict.
78–0	Insomnia, nervous, lacks self-confidence, verbal. Note: Scale 0 coded low was infrequently associated with lack of self-confidence.
78–1	Insomnia, nervous, lacks self-confidence.
78–2	Insomnia, nervous, lacks self-confidence. Note: Scale 2 coded low was infrequently associated with lack of self-confidence.
78–3	Insomnia, nervous, lacks self-confidence, cried in the interview.
78–4	Insomnia, nervous, lacks self-confidence.
78–5	Insomnia, nervous, headaches, exhaustion, anxieties, lacks self-confidence, indecisive, socially insecure, distractible in study.
78–6/9	Insomnia, nervous, lacks self-confidence.
78–X	Insomnia, headaches, nervous, exhaustion, depressed, lacks self-confidence, father conflict, mother conflict, sibling conflict, 8+ conferences, lacks skills with the opposite sex.
789–0	Insomnia, nervous, restless, exhaustion, lacks self-confidence, confused, 8+ conferences, verbal, resistant in the interview, sibling conflict, distractible in study, marriage oriented, socially extroverted. Note: Scale 0 coded low was infrequently associated with exhaustion, lack of self-confidence, confusion, sibling conflict.
789–1	Insomnia, nervous, restless, lacks self-confidence, confused, 8+ conferences, verbal, resistant in the interview, sibling conflict, distractible in study, vague goals, socially extroverted. Note: Scale 1 coded low was infrequently associated with sibling conflict.
789–2	Insomnia, nervous, restless, exhaustion, lacks self-confidence, confused, 8+ conferences, verbal, resistant in the interview, sibling conflict, distractible in study, socially extroverted. Note: Scale 2 coded low was infrequently associated with lack of self-confidence and confusion.
789–3	Insomnia, nervous, restless, lacks self-confidence, confused, 8+ conferences, verbal, resistant in the interview, cried in the interview, sibling conflict, distractible in study, vague goals.
789–4	Insomnia, nervous, restless, lacks self-confidence, confused, 8+ conferences, verbal, resistant in the interview, nonresponsive, sibling conflict, distractible in study, shy in the interview. Note: Scale 9 coded high was infrequently associated with shyness in the interview.

789–5	Insomnia, nervous, restless, headaches, exhaustion, anxieties, lacks self-confidence, confused, indecisive, 8+ conferences, verbal, resistant in the interview, wants answers, sibling conflict, distractible in study, socially insecure. Note: Scale 5 coded low was infrequently associated with resistance in the interview.
789–6	Insomnia, nervous, restless, lacks self-confidence, confused, 8+ conferences, verbal, resistant in the interview, sibling conflict, distractible in study.
789–X	Insomnia, nervous, restless, headaches, depressed, exhaustion, lacks self-confidence, confused, 8+ conferences, verbal, resistant in the interview, sibling conflict, father conflict, mother conflict, distractible in study, lacks skills with the opposite sex.
79–0	Nervous, exhaustion, confused, verbal, sibling conflict, distractible in study, marriage oriented, socially extroverted. Note: Scale 0 coded low was infrequently associated with exhaustion, confusion, sibling conflict.
79–1	Nervous, confused, sibling conflict, distractible in study, vague goals, socially extroverted. Note: Scale 1 coded low was infrequently associated with sibling conflict.
79–2	Nervous, confused, sibling conflict, distractible in study, socially extroverted. Note: Scale 2 coded low was infrequently associated with confusion.
79–3	Nervous, confused, cried in the interview, sibling conflict, distractible in study, vague goals.
79–4	Nervous, confused, nonresponsive, sibling conflict, distractible in study, shy in the interview. Note: Scale 9 coded high was infrequently associated with shyness in the interview.
79–5	Nervous, headaches, insomnia, exhaustion, anxieties, confused, indecisive, lacks self-confidence, verbal, sibling conflict, distractible in study, socially insecure.
79–6/8	Nervous, confused, sibling conflict, distractible in study.
79–X	Nervous, headaches, confused, sibling conflict, distractible in study.
8–0	Verbal.
8–5	Lacks academic drive, distractible in study.
8–X	Depressed, father conflict, mother conflict, sibling conflict, 8+ conferences, lacks skills with the opposite sex.
89–0	Restless, resistant in the interview, verbal, confused, 8+ conferences, socially extroverted, marriage oriented. Note: Scale 0 coded low was infrequently associated with confusion.
89–1	Restless, resistant in the interview, verbal, confused, 8+ conferences, socially extroverted, vague goals.
89–2	Restless, exhaustion, resistant in the interview, verbal, confused, 8+ conferences, socially extroverted. Note: Scale 2 coded low was infrequently associated with confusion.
89–3	Restless, resistant in the interview, verbal, confused, 8+ conferences, vague goals.
89–4	Restless, resistant in the interview, verbal, nonresponsive, confused, 8+ conferences, shy in the interview.
89–5	Restless, anxieties, exhaustion, resistant in the interview, verbal, wants answers, confused, 8+ conferences, distractible in study. Note: Scale

FEMALE SECTION

	5 coded low was infrequently associated with resistance in the interview.
89–6/7	Restless, resistant in the interview, verbal, confused, 8+ conferences.
89–X	Restless, depressed, resistant in the interview, verbal, confused, 8+ conferences, father conflict, mother conflict, sibling conflict, lacks skills with the opposite sex.
9–0	Marriage oriented, socially extroverted, verbal.
9–1	Vague goals, socially extroverted.
9–2	Socially extroverted.
9–3	Vague goals.
9–4	Shy in the interview, nonresponsive. Note: Scale 9 coded high was infrequently associated with shyness in the interview.
9–5	Verbal, exhaustion.

Appendix Tables and References

Table I. The MMPI Patterns Meeting Statistical Criteria of Significance That Were Shown by Male Students in Each of the Subgroups*

Subgroup	N	Pattern †	% of Total ‡	% of Subgroup	Diff §	C.R.
Vague goals	91	8 high 27		39	12	2.67
		78 paired high 12		20	8	2.42
Tense (not includ-	81	7 high 32		52	20	3.92
ing those in the		2 high 24		39	15	3.26
restless and		5 high 43		32	−11	2.04
nervous groups)		27 paired high 11		25	14	4.12
		78 paired high 12		26	14	4.00
		2–X 7		21	14	5.00
		5–0 21		11	−10	2.27
		7–X 11		21	10	2.94
		27–X 1		13	12	10.91
Lacks academic	73	2 high 24		12	−12	2.45
motivation		5 high 43		29	−14	2.46
		89–0 6		15	9	3.21
Indecisive	72	2 high 24		37	13	2.65
		7 high 32		57	25	4.63
		8 high 27		40	13	2.55
		9 high 38		26	−12	2.14
		07 high 3		10	7	3.68
		27 high 11		25	14	3.89
		78 high 12		25	13	3.42
		0 low 49		35	−14	2.46
		7–X 11		26	15	4.17
		8–X 8		21	13	4.19
		9–0 23		11	−12	2.50
		27–X 1		12	11	9.17
		78–X 5		17	12	4.80
Restless (not	72	3 high 33		21	−12	2.22
including those in		5 high 43		58	15	2.63
the tense and		0 low 49		36	−13	2.24
nervous groups)		3–0 24		11	−13	2.65
		5–1 8		18	10	3.22
One or no	80	3 high 33		47	14	2.74
interviews		0X paired low 16		24	8	2.00
		3–0 24		39	15	3.19
		7–0 10		22	12	3.64
		37–0 4		11	7	3.33
		38–0 4		10	6	2.86

* The codebook is built on Tables I and II and contains no data not given here. The data on male students have been previously published (3, 4, and 5); the authors are indebted to Dr. C. Gilbert Wrenn, editor of the *Journal of Counseling Psychology*, for his permission to reproduce the data.

† The patterns should be read as in the codebook section. A dash separates high codings from low codings; an X means "no scale."

‡ There were 2,634 students in the total male group.

§ A minus sign preceding the difference between the two percentages indicates that the designated pattern was less frequent in the subgroup than in the group of male students as a whole.

127

Table I — continued

Subgroup	N	Pattern	% of Total	% of Subgroup	Diff	C.R.
Aggressive or belligerent	58	4 high 25		38	13	2.32
		9 high 38		52	14	2.22
		29 paired high 3		10	7	3.18
		3–0 24		50	26	4.64
		4–0 15		26	11	2.39
		8–0 12		21	9	2.14
		9–0 23		40	17	3.14
		49–2 3		12	9	4.09
Four or more conferences	127	35 paired high 13		21	8	2.76
		1 low 15		21	6	2.00
Nonresponsive or nonverbal	55	7 high 32		49	17	2.74
		8 high 27		40	13	2.20
		9 high 38		25	−13	2.03
		78 paired high 12		22	10	2.32
		0 low 49		31	−18	2.69
		3–0 24		7	−17	2.98
		5–0 21		9	−12	2.22
		7–X 11		20	9	2.19
		7–1 5		14	9	3.10
		9–0 23		11	−12	2.14
		57–1 2		11	9	5.00
Father conflict	53	4–0 15		28	13	2.71
Wants answers or insists on test scores	52	5 high 43		29	−14	2.06
		0 low 49		65	16	2.32
		05 paired low 4		13	9	3.46
		3–0 24		40	16	2.71
Introverted or self-conscious or socially insecure	51	0 high 6		34	28	8.48
		2 high 24		44	20	3.39
		3 high 33		16	−17	2.61
		8 high 27		46	19	3.11
		9 high 38		24	−14	2.09
		02 paired high 3		24	21	8.75
		05 paired high 3		16	13	5.42
		07 paired high 3		12	9	3.75
		28 paired high 6		14	8	2.42
		78 paired high 12		22	10	2.22
		0 low 49		14	−35	5.07
		9 low 13		24	11	2.34
		0–1 2		14	12	6.31
		0–9 2		12	10	5.26
		2–X 7		18	11	3.05
		3–0 24		6	−18	3.05
		5–0 21		6	−15	2.68
		8–9 3		12	9	3.91
		9–0 23		8	−15	2.59
		27–X 1		12	11	7.86
Sibling conflict	50	7–X 11		20	9	2.04

Table I — continued

Subgroup	N	Pattern	% of Total	% of Subgroup	Diff	C.R.
Nonverbal or	49	0 low 49	49	33	−16	2.25
nonrelator		3–0 24	24	10	−14	2.33
		9–0 23	23	10	−13	2.17
Shy or withdrawn	48	0 high 6	6	29	23	6.76
in the interview		05 paired high 3	3	12	9	3.75
		07 paired high 3	3	14	11	4.58
		0 low 49	49	23	−26	3.61
		9–0 23	23	8	−15	2.50
Lacks social skills	39	0 high 6	6	20	14	3.68
		2 high 24	24	38	14	2.06
		3 high 33	33	15	−18	2.40
		02 paired high 3	3	13	10	3.70
		0 low 49	49	23	−26	3.25
		3–0 24	24	8	−16	2.88
		27–X 1	1	10	9	5.62
Tense on	37	1 high 11	11	22	11	2.17
examinations		2 high 24	24	43	19	2.75
		7 high 32	32	49	17	2.24
		27 paired high 11	11	24	13	2.55
		29 paired high 3	3	13	10	3.57
		27–1 1	1	11	10	5.88
Home dependency	36	15 paired high 3	3	14	11	3.92
		35 paired high 13	13	28	15	2.68
Unrealistic or	34	5 high 43	43	23	−20	2.38
illogical		3–0 24	24	9	−15	2.05
Lacks knowledge	32	8 high 27	27	44	17	2.18
or information		38 paired high 5	5	19	14	3.68
		78 paired high 12	12	28	16	2.85
		7–0 10	10	28	18	3.40
		8–0 12	12	25	13	2.28
		38–0 4	4	16	12	3.53
		78–0 3	3	16	13	4.33
Depressed or	32	2 high 24	24	56	32	4.26
unhappy		7 high 32	32	56	24	2.92
		07 paired high 3	3	12	9	3.00
		27 paired high 11	11	37	26	4.73
		0 low 49	49	22	−27	3.07
		2–X 7	7	28	21	4.67
		3–0 24	24	9	−15	2.00
		7–X 11	11	28	17	3.09
		8–X 8	8	25	17	3.54
		27–X 1	1	19	18	10.00
		78–X 5	5	19	14	3.69
		28–X 3	3	16	13	4.33
Confused	31	7 high 32	32	52	20	2.40
		8 high 27	27	52	25	3.16
		78 paired high 12	12	29	17	2.93
		7–X 11	11	26	15	2.68

Table I — continued

Subgroup	N	Pattern	% of Total	% of Subgroup	Diff	C.R.
		8–X 8		26	18	3.75
		1X paired low 2		10	8	3.33
		27–1 1		10	9	5.00
		58–X 2		13	11	4.58
		89–X 1		10	9	5.00
Dependent	31	27–9 2		10	8	3.33
Poor rapport	31	59 paired high 16		35	19	2.92
		0 low 49		29	−20	2.25
		1X paired low ... 2		10	8	3.33
		47–X 2		10	8	3.33
Mother conflict	31	3 high 33		6	−27	3.21
		5 high 43		61	18	2.04
		07 paired high 3		13	10	3.22
		59 paired high 16		35	19	2.92
		3–0 24		6	−18	2.37
		7–X 11		26	15	2.68
		27–X 1		10	9	4.99
		59–0 9		22	13	2.55
Worries a great deal	30	2 high 24		57	33	4.28
		7 high 32		57	25	2.94
		9 high 38		17	−21	2.39
		25 paired high 9		20	11	2.11
		27 paired high 11		43	32	5.61
		28 paired high 6		20	14	3.18
		46 paired high 2		10	8	3.33
		0 low 49		26	−23	2.85
		9X paired low ... 3		13	10	3.22
		2–X 7		37	30	6.52
		7–X 11		33	22	3.86
		8–X 8		23	15	3.06
		25–X 2		13	11	4.58
		27–X 1		33	32	16.84
		28–X.......... 3		20	17	5.48
		78–X 5		17	12	3.08
Nervous (not including those in the tense and restless groups)	28	3–0 24		7	−17	2.12
Wants reassurance only	28	25 paired high 9		21	12	2.22
		57 paired high 11		25	14	2.37
		4 low 11		28	17	2.88
		7 low 7		25	18	3.79
		07 paired low 3		14	11	3.44
		49 paired low 2		14	12	4.61
		25–9 2		11	9	3.46
Shy or lacks skills with the opposite sex	26	2 high 24		50	26	3.13
		4 high 25		8	−17	2.02
		9 high 38		11	−27	2.84

Table I — continued

Subgroup	N	Pattern	% of Total	% of Subgroup	Diff	C.R.
		28 paired high	6	27	21	4.47
		0 low	49	23	−26	2.65
		2–X	7	31	24	4.70
		5–0	21	4	−17	2.12
		7–X	11	27	16	2.62
		25–X	2	11	9	3.33
		27–X	1	23	22	11.00
		28–X	3	19	16	4.85
		35–X	2	11	9	3.33
		78–X	5	19	14	3.26
Rationalizes a great deal	24	29 paired high	3	19	16	4.57
		9–6	7	21	14	2.69
		29–0	1	12	11	5.24
		49–6	2	12	10	3.57
Defensive	23	79 paired high	8	22	14	2.50
Insomnia	23	2 high	24	43	19	2.13
		3 high	33	13	−20	2.04
		7 high	32	56	24	2.47
		25 paired high	9	22	13	2.16
		27 paired high	11	35	24	3.69
		28 paired high	6	26	20	4.00
		2–X	7	43	36	6.79
		5–X	8	22	14	2.50
		7–X	11	39	28	4.31
		8–X	8	30	22	3.93
		25–X	2	22	20	7.14
		27–X	1	35	34	16.19
		28–X	3	26	23	6.57
		78–X	5	22	17	3.77
Home conflict	20	7 high	32	60	28	2.66
		47 paired high	5	20	15	3.06
		57 paired high	11	25	14	2.00
		58 paired high	8	20	12	2.00
		79 paired high	8	20	12	2.00
		1X paired low . . .	2	15	13	4.33
		5–X	8	20	12	2.00
		7–1	5	20	15	3.06
		15–4	1	10	9	3.91
		27–X	1	10	9	3.91
		45–1	1	10	9	3.91
		57–1	2	15	13	4.33
		79–1	1	10	9	3.91

Table II. The MMPI Patterns Meeting Statistical Criteria of Significance That Were Shown by Female Students in Each of the Supgroups *

Subgroup	N	Pattern †	% of Total ‡	% of Subgroup	Diff §	C.R.
Tense	48	2 low 22	6	−16		2.71
Marriage oriented	95	3 high 26	39	13		3.02
		39 paired high 7	15	8		3.20
		3–0 14	24	10		2.94
		9–0 17	26	9		2.43
		0 low 34	45	11		2.34
Mother conflict	52	3–X 3	13	10		4.35
		2–9 3	10	7		3.04
		8–X 6	19	13		4.06
		38–X 1	10	9		6.92
		X low 12	27	15		3.41
Lacks academic drive	61	4 high 27	43	16		2.86
		34 paired high 7	18	11		3.44
		3–0 14	26	12		2.79
		4–0 13	24	11		2.62
		37–0 3	10	7		3.33
		45–0 2	10	8		4.44
		0 low 34	52	18		3.00
		2 low 22	11	−11		2.11
Socially insecure (not including those in the shy group)	31	0 high 15	32	17		2.70
		3 high 26	10	−16		2.05
		7 high 33	52	19		2.26
		2 high 17	35	18		2.69
		4 high 27	10	−17		2.15
		07 paired high 6	22	16		3.81
		29 paired high 3	13	10		3.33
		27 paired high 8	22	14		2.92
		0–3 3	13	10		3.33
		7–5 13	29	16		2.20
		2–5 8	22	14		2.92
		2–6 2	10	8		3.20
		07–9 1	10	9		5.29
		07–5 3	13	10		3.33
		0 low 34	10	−24		2.86
		2 low 22	6	−16		2.16
Rebellious toward home	21	5 high 24	5	−19		2.04
		4 high 27	52	25		2.60
		47 paired high 7	24	17		3.09
		4–5 9	33	24		3.93
Physical inferiority	21	0 high 15	33	18		2.34
		2 high 17	43	26		3.21

* These data on female students have not previously been published.

† The patterns should be read as in the codebook section. A dash separates high codings from low codings; an X means "no scale."

‡ There were 1,564 students in the total female group.

§ A minus sign preceding the difference between the two percentages indicates that the designated pattern was less frequent in the subgroup than in the group of female students as a whole.

Table II — continued

Subgroup	N	Pattern	% of Total	% of Subgroup	Diff	C.R.
		06 paired high	4	19	15	3.57
		6–5	9	28	19	3.11
		2–1	4	24	20	4.76
		06–5	1	14	13	6.19
		02–1	2	14	12	3.87
		26–1	1	14	13	6.19
Anxieties	20	5 high	24	5	−19	2.00
		2 high	17	60	43	5.18
		37 paired high	7	20	13	2.28
		27 paired high	8	25	17	2.83
		26 paired high	3	15	12	3.16
		24 paired high	4	35	31	7.21
		28 paired high	5	20	15	3.12
		7–5	13	35	22	2.97
		2–5	8	45	37	6.17
		4–5	9	25	16	2.54
		8–5	10	30	20	2.98
		37–0	3	15	12	3.16
		27–5	4	20	16	3.72
		78–5	5	20	15	3.12
		26–5	2	15	13	4.06
		24–5	2	25	23	7.19
		28–5	2	20	18	5.62
		5 low	29	65	36	3.56
Lacks skills with the opposite sex	24	0 high	15	42	27	3.75
		2 high	17	50	33	4.34
		02 paired high	5	21	16	3.64
		24 paired high	4	17	13	3.33
		28 paired high	5	21	16	3.64
		0–X	2	12	10	3.45
		0–1	5	21	16	3.64
		2–X	3	17	14	4.00
		2–5	8	25	17	3.09
		4–5	9	21	12	2.07
		8–X	6	21	15	3.12
		0 low	34	4	−30	3.12
		2 low	22	4	−18	2.14
		02–1	2	12	10	3.45
		24–5	2	17	15	5.17
		28–X	2	12	10	3.45
8+ conferences	32	5 high	24	9	−15	2.00
		6 high	25	47	22	2.89
		8 high	30	50	20	2.50
		78 paired high	11	22	11	2.04
		26 paired high	3	16	13	4.33
		68 paired high	6	22	16	3.90
		6–X	3	16	13	4.33
		8–X	6	19	13	3.17
		X low	12	25	13	2.28
		68–X	1	12	11	6.47

Table II — continued

Subgroup	N	Pattern	% of Total	% of Subgroup	Diff	C.R.
Vague goals	21	9 high 37	62	25	2.38
		59 paired high 9	24	15	2.46
		49 paired high 10	24	14	2.15
		9–1 10	24	14	2.15
		9–3 4	24	20	4.76
		4–6 3	19	16	4.32
		79–1 2	14	12	4.00
		79–3 1	14	13	6.50
		49–6 1	14	13	6.50
		45–6 1	14	13	6.50
Sibling conflict	39	7 high 33	49	16	2.16
		79 paired high 9	20	11	2.44
		7–X 6	18	12	3.24
		8–X 6	18	12	3.24
		0 low 34	18	−16	2.13
		1 low 22	8	−14	2.12
		79–5 3	13	10	3.70
Indecisive	37	0 high 15	27	12	2.07
		2 high 17	35	18	2.95
		24 paired high 4	16	12	3.87
		2–5 8	22	14	3.18
		4–5 9	22	13	2.83
		7–5 13	24	11	2.00
		5 low 29	46	17	2.30
		2 low 22	3	−19	2.83
		24–5 2	11	9	3.91
Dependent	37	5 low 29	46	17	2.30
Father conflict	32	5 high 24	9	−15	2.00
		2 high 17	31	14	2.12
		8 high 30	50	20	2.50
		04 paired high 1	12	11	6.47
		3–X 3	12	9	3.00
		9–X 4	19	15	3.17
		2 low 22	6	−16	2.22
Depressed	32	7 high 33	50	17	2.07
		5 high 24	6	−18	2.40
		2 high 17	41	24	3.64
		8 high 30	50	20	2.50
		27 paired high 8	28	20	4.25
		24 paired high 4	19	15	4.41
		28 paired high 5	22	17	4.47
		48 paired high 9	25	16	3.20
		2–X 3	12	9	3.00
		2–5 8	25	17	3.62
		8–X 6	19	13	3.17
		27–5 4	22	18	5.29
		0 low 34	6	−28	3.37
Nonverbal	31	0 high 15	32	17	2.70
		08 paired high 3	22	19	6.33

Table II — continued

Subgroup	N	Pattern	% of Total	% of Subgroup	Diff	C.R.
		0–X	2	10	8	3.20
		2–6	2	10	8	3.20
		08–5	1	10	9	5.29
Headaches	30	1 high	6	23	17	3.95
		5 high	24	7	−17	2.21
		1–5	2	13	11	4.23
		3–5	9	33	24	4.61
		7–X	6	20	14	3.25
		7–5	13	27	14	2.29
		13–5	2	10	8	3.08
		37–5	3	13	10	3.22
		38–5	2	10	8	3.08
		48–X	2	10	8	3.08
		1 low	22	0	−22	2.93
		5 low	29	53	24	2.93
		2 low	22	3	−19	2.53
Tense on examinations	30	3 high	26	47	21	2.66
		3–X	3	13	10	3.22
		3–0	14	27	13	2.06
		2–0	2	10	8	3.08
		2–5	8	20	12	2.45
		02–5	2	10	8	3.08
		36–0	3	13	10	3.22
		47–X	1	10	9	5.29
Confused	29	79 paired high	9	24	15	2.88
		78 paired high	11	27	16	2.81
		0 low	34	10	−24	2.76
		2 low	22	3	−19	2.50
Insomnia	29	7 high	33	59	26	3.02
		37 paired high	7	24	17	3.62
		47 paired high	7	24	17	3.62
		78 paired high	11	24	13	2.00
		48 paired high	9	21	12	2.31
		3–5	9	21	12	2.31
		7–5	13	41	28	4.52
		37–0	3	14	11	3.55
		37–5	3	17	14	4.52
		47–X	1	10	9	5.00
		48–X	2	14	12	4.61
		1 low	22	3	−19	2.50
Verbal	29	8 high	30	48	18	2.14
		49 paired high	10	24	14	2.54
		89 paired high	11	24	13	2.28
		38 paired high	5	17	12	3.00
		9–0	17	31	14	2.03
		9–5	10	21	11	2.00
		3–X	3	14	11	3.55
		8–0	9	27	18	3.46
		49–0	6	21	15	3.41
		48–0	4	17	13	3.71

Table II — continued

Subgroup	N	Pattern	% of Total	% of Subgroup	Diff	C.R.
		48–5	3	14	11	3.55
		38–0	2	10	8	3.08
Lacks self-confidence	29	0 high	15	38	23	3.54
		7 high	33	59	26	3.02
		2 high	17	45	28	4.06
		07 paired high	6	21	15	3.41
		02 paired high	5	21	16	4.00
		29 paired high	3	14	11	3.55
		27 paired high	8	27	19	3.80
		78 paired high	11	27	16	2.50
		7–5	13	31	18	2.90
		2–1	4	17	13	3.71
		2–6	2	14	12	4.61
		2–4	1	10	9	5.00
		0 low	34	10	−24	2.76
		2 low	22	3	−19	2.50
Socially shy (not including those in the socially insecure group)	28	0 high	15	57	42	6.27
		5 high	24	7	−17	2.12
		2 high	17	43	26	3.71
		09 paired high	3	14	11	3.44
		07 paired high	6	25	19	4.32
		06 paired high	4	18	14	3.89
		02 paired high	5	25	20	5.00
		08 paired high	3	14	11	3.44
		27 paired high	8	25	17	3.33
		0–X	2	11	9	3.33
		0–9	4	18	14	3.89
		0–5	5	28	23	5.75
		2–5	8	21	13	2.55
		09–1	1	11	10	5.55
		07–2	1	11	10	5.55
		07–4	1	11	10	5.55
		02–5	2	14	12	4.44
		08–5	1	11	10	5.55
		27–9	2	11	9	3.33
		0 low	34	0	−34	3.82
		2 low	22	3	−19	2.43
Exhaustion	27	2 high	17	33	16	2.25
		8 high	30	48	18	2.07
		9–5	10	22	12	2.17
		3–5	9	22	13	2.41
		7–5	13	30	17	2.66
		39–5	2	13	11	4.07
		79–0	3	13	10	3.03
		79–5	3	13	10	3.03
		89–5	3	13	10	3.03
		89–2	3	13	10	3.03
		37–5	3	15	12	3.64
		78–X	2	13	11	3.40
		0 low	34	15	−19	2.11
		1 low	22	4	−18	2.28

Table II — continued

Subgroup	N	Pattern	% of Total	% of Subgroup	Diff	C.R.
Overprotective mother	26	8 high	30	50	20	2.25
		48 paired high	9	35	26	4.64
Nonresponsive	25	3 high	26	8	−18	2.07
		2 high	17	32	15	2.03
		4 high	27	4	−23	2.61
		5X paired high . . .	4	16	12	3.16
		9–4	4	16	12	3.16
		26–5	2	12	10	3.57
Nervous (not including those in the tense and restless groups)	23	08 paired high	3	17	14	3.89
		79 paired high	9	22	13	2.20
		78 paired high	11	26	15	2.09
		7–5	13	35	22	3.19
		2–5	8	22	14	2.50
		37–5	3	17	14	3.89
		1 low	22	4	−18	2.09
		5 low	29	52	23	2.45
Home conflict	22	4 high	27	54	27	2.87
		49 paired high	10	23	13	2.06
		34 paired high	7	27	20	3.70
		3–5	9	23	14	2.33
		49–X	1	14	13	6.50
		0 low	34	14	−20	2.00
		2 low	22	4	−18	2.04
Wants answers	22	2–5	8	23	15	2.63
		89–5	3	14	11	3.05
Resistant in the interview	22	89 paired high	11	27	16	2.43
		6–0	8	23	15	2.63
		89–1	2	14	12	4.00
		5 low	29	9	−20	2.08
Distractible in study	22	2 high	17	43	26	3.21
		8 high	30	57	27	2.73
		79 paired high	9	24	15	2.46
		27 paired high	8	24	16	2.71
		28 paired high	5	24	19	4.04
		3–5	9	24	15	2.46
		5–X	2	14	12	3.87
		8–5	10	28	18	2.77
		38–5	2	19	17	5.48
		X low	12	28	16	2.28
4 to 7 conferences	30	2 high	17	25	8	2.67
		27 paired high	8	17	9	4.28
		2 low	22	15	−7	2.12
Socially extroverted	20	9 high	37	75	38	3.55
		39 paired high	7	25	18	3.16
		59 paired high	9	25	16	2.54
		49 paired high	10	45	35	5.22
		9–0	17	65	48	5.78
		9–1	10	30	20	2.98

Table II — continued

Subgroup	N	Pattern	% of Total	% of Subgroup	Diff	C.R.
		9–2 12	45	33	4.58	
		3–0 14	40	26	3.38	
		3–2 6	20	14	2.64	
		5–0 11	30	19	2.75	
		6–0 8	25	17	2.83	
		6–2 5	20	15	3.12	
		4–0 13	45	32	4.32	
		4–1 5	20	15	3.12	
		4–2 5	25	20	4.17	
		39–0 5	20	15	3.12	
		59–0 5	20	15	3.12	
		49–0 6	45	39	7.36	
		49–1 2	20	18	5.62	
		49–2 3	25	22	5.76	
		0 low 34	85	51	4.86	
		2 low 22	50	28	3.04	
Shy in the interview	50	0 high 15	34	19	3.80	
		9 high 37	20	−17	2.50	
		6 high 25	42	17	2.83	
		4 high 27	12	−15	2.42	
		08 paired high 3	14	11	4.58	
		0–5 5	14	9	3.00	
		9–4 4	14	10	3.70	
		6–4 3	12	9	3.75	
		0 low 34	14	−20	3.03	
Restless (not including those in the nervous or tense groups)	48	9 high 37	52	15	2.17	
		89 paired high 11	25	14	3.18	
		6–X 3	12	9	3.60	
Cried in the interview	79	7–3 3	10	7	3.68	

REFERENCES

1. Cronbach, L. J., and P. E. Meehl. "Construct validity in psychological tests." *Psychol. Bull.*, 1955, 52, 281–302.
2. Drake, L. E. "Scale 0 (Social Introversion)." In G. S. Welsh and W. G. Dahlstrom, eds., *Basic readings on the MMPI in psychology and medicine.* Minneapolis: Univ. of Minnesota Press, 1956.
3. Drake, L. E. "MMPI profiles and interview behavior." In G. S. Welsh and W. G. Dahlstrom, eds., *Basic readings on the MMPI in psychology and medicine.* Minneapolis: Univ. of Minnesota Press, 1956.
4. Drake, L. E. "Interpretation of MMPI profiles in counseling male clients." *J. counsel. Psychol.*, 1956, 3, 83–88.
5. Drake, L. E., and E. R. Oetting. "An MMPI pattern and a suppressor variable predictive of academic achievement." *J. counsel. Psychol.*, 1957, 4, 245–247.
6. Drake, L. E., and W. B. Thiede. "Further validation of Scale 0 (Si)." In G. S. Welsh and W. G. Dahlstrom, eds., *Basic readings on the MMPI in psychology and medicine.* Minneapolis: Univ. of Minnesota Press, 1956.
7. Hathaway, S. R. "A coding system for MMPI profile classification." In G. S. Welsh and W. G. Dahlstrom, eds., *Basic readings on the MMPI in psychology and medicine.* Minneapolis: Univ. of Minnesota Press, 1956.
8. Hathaway, S. R. "Scales 5 (Masculinity-Femininity), 6 (Paranoia), and 8 (Schizophrenia)." In G. S. Welsh and W. G. Dahlstrom, eds., *Basic readings on the MMPI in psychology and medicine.* Minneapolis: Univ. of Minnesota Press, 1956.
9. Hathaway, S. R., and J. C. McKinley. "Scale 2 (Depression)." In G. S. Welsh and W. G. Dahlstrom, eds., *Basic readings on the MMPI in psychology and medicine.* Minneapolis: Univ. of Minnesota Press, 1956.
10. Hathaway, S. R., and P. E. Meehl. *An atlas for the clinical use of the MMPI.* Minneapolis: Univ. of Minnesota Press, 1952.
11. Hathaway, S. R., and E. D. Monachesi. *Analyzing and predicting juvenile delinquency with the MMPI.* Minneapolis: Univ. of Minnesota Press, 1953.
12. McKinley, J. C., and S. R. Hathaway. "Scale 1 (Hypochondriasis)." In G. S. Welsh and W. G. Dahlstrom, eds., *Basic readings on the MMPI in psychology and medicine.* Minneapolis: Univ. of Minnesota Press, 1956.
13. McKinley, J. C., and S. R. Hathaway. "Scales 3 (Hysteria), 9 (Hypomania), and 4 (Psychopathic Deviate)." In G. S. Welsh and W. G. Dahlstrom, eds., *Basic readings on the MMPI in psychology and medicine.* Minneapolis: Univ. of Minnesota Press, 1956.
14. McKinley, J. C., and S. R. Hathaway. "Scale 7 (Psychasthenia)." In G. S. Welsh and W. G. Dahlstrom, eds., *Basic readings on the MMPI in psychology and medicine.* Minneapolis: Univ. of Minnesota Press, 1956.
15. McKinley, J. C., S. R. Hathaway, and P. E. Meehl. "The K Scale." In G. S.

REFERENCES

Welsh and W. G. Dahlstrom, eds., *Basic readings on the MMPI in psychology and medicine.* Minneapolis: Univ. of Minnesota Press, 1956.

16. Meehl, P. E. *Clinical versus statistical prediction.* Minneapolis: Univ. of Minnesota Press, 1954.
17. Meehl, P. E., and S. R. Hathaway. "The K Factor as a suppressor variable in the MMPI." In G. S. Welsh and W. G. Dahlstrom, eds., *Basic readings on the MMPI in psychology and medicine.* Minneapolis: Univ. of Minnesota Press, 1956.
18. Meehl, P. E., and Albert Rosen. "Antecedent probability and the efficiency of psychometric signs, patterns, or cutting scores." *Psychol. Bull.*, 1955, 52, 194–216.
19. Super, D. E. *Appraising vocational fitness.* New York: Harper and Brothers, 1949.